ROOTED & GROUNDED IN LOVE

ABSORBING KEY NUTRIENTS TO BECOMING A STRONG BELIEVER

THE ANTHOLOGY

Rooted and Grounded in Love
Absorbing Key Nutrients to Becoming a Strong Believer

The Anthology

Published by Kingdom Publishing, LLC
Printed in the United States of America
Odenton, MD 21113

ISBN: 978-1-967006-01-4

Table of Contents

Author

Antonio Palmer

Apostle Antonio M. Palmer is the Senior Pastor of Kingdom Celebration Center and the Presiding Bishop of Kingdom Alliance of Churches International, overseeing a global network of 74 churches. With a ministry rooted in the Gospel since 1993, he planted his first church in Annapolis, Maryland, in 1995 and became a beacon of leadership, service, and transformation.

A passionate advocate for missions, Bishop Palmer leads leadership conferences, plants churches, and provides humanitarian aid to thousands of children in need across the globe. His work includes substantial financial support for orphanages in India and East Africa, demonstrating a steadfast commitment to serving the underserved.

Bishop Palmer, a respected community leader, is celebrated for fostering unity and collaboration among diverse groups. His efforts address critical issues, promote meaningful dialogue, and inspire transformative change. He holds a Bachelor of Divinity and a Master's in Pastoral Counseling. He has been recognized with numerous accolades, including two Governor Citations, two County Executive Citations, and the prestigious Martin Luther King Jr. Drum Major Award.

As an entrepreneur, Bishop Palmer owns Kingdom Publishing LLC, Antonio Marlin Art, and Kingdom Kare, Inc., a thriving nonprofit organization. He is also the author of seven impactful books: *Living By the Spirit, Love Thyself: Empowering Men for Healthy Living, God's Rest Revealed: A Life Flowing with Milk and Honey, Building an Effective Prayer Life, Mark the Perfect Man: How to Find a Model of Maturity, Revival: God Will Come Where You Are,* and *Little Kairo Takes on the World* (Children's Book).

INTRODUCTION

The foundation of our faith walk is *love*—God's love for us, our love for Him, and our love for one another. The Apostle Paul's prayer in Ephesians 3:14-21 is a profound intercession, asking that we be strengthened by the Spirit, that Christ may dwell in our hearts through faith, and that we be *rooted and grounded in agape (love)*. The Messiah's love surpasses all things—it is the greatest truth we will ever know and understand. Paul prayed for us to be rooted and grounded in it because this love seeks our ultimate good, has our best interest at heart, keeps us constantly on His mind, and will do anything to reach us. It is overwhelming, never-ending, unfailing, and even reckless in its pursuit of us.

In 1 Corinthians 13:4-8, Paul describes love—*agape*—as the most excellent way. This love is patient and kind. It does not envy, boast, or behave unseemly. It seeks not its own, is not easily provoked, and does not rejoice in iniquity but in the truth. Love bears all things, believes all things, hopes all things, and endures all things. Love never fails. These attributes serve as the rich nutrients that sustain and nourish the believer's soul.

The Hebrew Scriptures (Tanakh) introduce us to *chesed*—God's covenantal, faithful, and committed love. This is the steadfast, enduring love that declares Yahweh's devotion to His people, a love that is better than life itself. Then there is *ahavah*—a love that is affectionate and active, one that calls us to love the Lord our God with all our heart, soul, and might, and to love our neighbors as ourselves. Jesus affirmed this as the greatest commandment, emphasizing that love is not merely a feeling but a pursuit, an action, and a way of being. Ahavah is often used to describe God's love for His people, a steadfast love that remains regardless of circumstances (Deuteronomy 7:7-8).

> *"The Lord did not set his love upon you, nor choose you, because ye were more in number than any people; for ye were the fewest of all people: but because the Lord loved you, and because he would keep the oath which he had sworn unto your fathers, hath the Lord brought you out with a mighty hand, and redeemed you out of the house of bondmen, from the hand of Pharaoh king of Egypt."*

The Greek word for love used in Ephesians 3:14-21 is *agape*—a selfless, sacrificial love that seeks the highest good of another without motive for personal gain. This love is a pursuit that requires intentional seeking. It is a behavior demonstrated through action. Agape love does not merely see a person as they are but envisions them as they ought to be. It calls us to perceive others through the eyes of Christ, beyond their present state, and to nurture them towards their God-ordained purpose.

What does it mean for believers to be *rooted and grounded in love?* It means continually drawing spiritual nourishment from God's love, which promotes growth in faith, character, and spiritual maturity. Like a building with a solid foundation, being grounded in God's love provides security and stability. It means feeling safe in His unwavering love, regardless of external circumstances. It conveys the idea that God's love is deeply integrated into a person's life, influencing their thoughts, actions, and interactions with others. This consistency reflects a life aligned with the principles of love, compassion, and grace.

The Greek words *rhizoo* and *themelioo* help us grasp the depth of being rooted and grounded. Rhizoo means to cause to strike root, to strengthen with roots, to become stable and unwavering. Themelioo means to lay a firm foundation, implying that our lives must be built on the truth of God's love.

1. To be rooted, we must have healthy roots—roots that grasp, comprehend, and hold onto the right substance for spiritual

nourishment. Without roots, a plant cannot be established and will wither away.

2. The roots must latch onto the right source in order to function at full capacity for the benefit of the tree.

3. Where we are planted is crucial. Psalm 1:3 declares that those who delight in the Lord are *like a tree planted by the rivers of water, bringing forth fruit in season, whose leaves will not wither, and whatever they do shall prosper.*

A root functions in several vital ways:

- **Absorption**: Just as a plant absorbs water and nutrients for its survival, our faith takes in God's love into our hearts.
- **Aeration**: Just as plant roots need oxygen to stay healthy, our spirits need the breath of God to remain alive and growing.
- **Food Storage**: Psalm 119:11 states, *"Thy word have I hid (stored) in my heart, that I might not sin against thee."*
- **Anchorage and Support**: Deep roots provide stability. Outward success means little without inward, internal growth. We must be deeply rooted in God's love to sustain any external achievements.

The soil is essential for the life of the tree. It provides the necessary nutrients and water for growth. When we are planted in the soil of God's love *(agape),* we will have an unfailing supply of life from the Spirit. This book will explore the transformative power of God's love, guiding us to understand, receive, and walk in the fullness of what it means to be *rooted and grounded* in Him. As we journey through Scripture, we will uncover the depth of His love and the call to love others as He loves us. This book will serve as volume 1, and will discuss eight of the 16 nutrients of God's love found in 1 Corinthians 13. May this revelation empower us to bear much fruit, living lives that reflect the heart of God to the world.

Authors

Phillip & Jacqueline Duncan

Apostle Phillip G. Duncan and Pastor Jacqueline Duncan are a devoted couple committed to advancing God's Kingdom. Together, they lead In His Presence Praise and Worship Center, a growing church they founded in 2008, where the Spirit of the Lord transforms lives.

Apostle Phillip, a passionate leader, challenges the Body of Christ to live with dominion and kingdom authority. A retired Marine Corps veteran, he leads ministries like Kingdom Leadership Academy and Men of Purpose, empowering future leaders and men to fulfill their God-given roles. Since their marriage in 1998, he and Pastor Jacqueline have worked together to mentor and train leaders.

Pastor Jacqueline is dedicated to empowering women to reach their full potential in Christ. As a life coach and mentor, she founded Sisters Enhancing Sisters (SES) to support women's growth through community and workshops. She also leads events like Women of Purpose and Leading Ladies of Integrity, helping women embrace Godly influence.

Together, the Duncans exemplify leadership, love, and service in their ministry. They are proud parents of two children, Shekinah and Jammar, and reside in Maryland.

Chapter 1
THE NUTRIENT OF SUPERNATURAL PATIENCE

"Love is patient."
(1 Corinthians 13:4)

In life, it's vital to recognize the season you are in. What is unfolding around you? Why are these circumstances presenting themselves? Have you ever pressed in with all your might, only to feel as though nothing is changing? Why do challenges seem to multiply? If you're asking these questions, you're not alone. Today, I want to share a profound message about supernatural patience—a crucial aspect of your spiritual journey. This is a season where God is cultivating your supernatural patience.

Patience Defined

The Greek term for patience is *hupomeno,* which translates to "to remain" or "to tarry behind." To remain is to abide, to endure under misfortune, to hold fast to one's faith in Christ amidst trials. When challenges press against you, when principalities come knocking at your door, this is where *hupomeno* shines. It means holding fast bravely, enduring with supernatural strength.

Patience is the capacity to accept or tolerate delay, trouble, or suffering without getting angry or upset. It's more than just waiting; it's about maintaining calm and composure in the face of adversity. To truly understand patience, we must explore its related concepts: tolerance and endurance.

The Old Testament presents patience as a wise and virtuous choice. Proverbs 19:11 explains, "A person's wisdom yields patience; it is to one's glory to overlook an offense." Being patient is tied to having self-control, understanding, and the ability to calm a quarrel.

The New Testament Greek word for patience, *"makrothymia,"* combines the words *"makros"* (long) and *"thumos"* (soul, heart). To be patient is to be "long souled," maintaining calm and perseverance even when tempted to give up. The Greek word, *"hypomone,"* describes patience toward circumstances, while *"makrothymia"* typically refers to patience toward people.

This perspective encourages us to think long-term, focusing on enduring challenges with a sense of purpose and steadiness, rather than seeking immediate solutions.

God's patience toward us is the ultimate example of long-suffering.

- **2 Peter 3:9**: "[God] is patient with you, not wanting anyone to perish, but everyone to come to repentance."
- **1 Timothy 1:16**: "I was shown mercy so that in me, the worst of sinners, Christ Jesus might display his immense patience as an example for those who would believe in him and receive eternal life."

God's patience is not just an attribute; it's the reason for our salvation. Through His patience, He allows us to repent and grow in faith.

As believers, we are called to emulate God's patience in our interactions with others:

- **Ephesians 4:2**: "Be completely humble and gentle; be patient, bearing with one another in love."
- **2 Timothy 4:2**: "Preach the word; be prepared in season and out of season; correct, rebuke and encourage—with great patience and careful instruction."

When we truly love others, we display patience in our relationships because, as **1 Corinthians 13:4** reminds us, "Love is patient."

The Importance of Patience

Supernatural patience is not merely a passive state; it must be actively cultivated. This patience equips you to find rest amid the turmoil. God calls us to "Be still and know that I am God," inviting us to trust Him fully and to learn how to operate in this divine patience. Our impatience often stems from a desire for immediate results but know this: God is building your patience for a reason.

Remember, patience is not merely the ability to wait; it's how we act while waiting. The Bible tells us that patience is from the Holy Spirit working in us. Because supernatural patience comes from God. It does not flow from us, but it flows from God.

Galatians 5:22-23 states, "But the fruit of the spirit is love, joy, peace, longsuffering, kindness, goodness, faithfulness, gentleness, and self-control. Against such, there is no law."

The Holy Spirit works in us by bringing the truth of God's Word. The Holy Spirit uses God's Word to cut through the lies of the world and it reveals the truth upon which we can stand.

The journey of life is not a race won by the swift or the strong; it belongs to those who endure to the end. Without supernatural patience, you risk missing the beauty of the moment.

Consider the process of earning a college degree. If you focus solely on the challenges and discomfort, you might find the journey unbearable. Yet, when you walk across that stage, diploma in hand, the pain of the process is overshadowed by the joy of accomplishment.

Patience is also a sign of wisdom. The Bible teaches that it is a virtue to overlook offenses and control one's temper.

- **Proverbs 19:11**: "A person's wisdom yields patience; it is to one's glory to overlook an offense."
- **Proverbs 14:29**: "Whoever is patient has great understanding, but one who is quick-tempered displays folly."
- **Proverbs 16:32**: "Better a patient person than a warrior, one with self-control than one who takes a city."

These scriptures highlight the importance of self-control, thoughtful response, and the wisdom of being slow to anger. Patience allows us to act with clarity and understanding rather than impulsive reactions.

Patience is often called a virtue because it reflects an inner strength and character aligned with God's nature. It is a sign of spiritual maturity when we trust God's timing and resist the urge to react hastily.

Think of life like sailing a boat on a river. Impatience is like heavy baggage you're carrying on board, slowing you down and making the journey more difficult. They're like burdensome luggage that might seem familiar and comfortable, but they weigh you down. Now, virtues are like favorable winds propelling your boat forward. Focusing on virtues is akin to adjusting your sails to catch the wind, making the journey smoother and more enjoyable. When we follow Jesus, it's like entrusting our navigation to a skilled captain.

Proverbs 3:6 encourages us to "acknowledge him in all your ways, and he will make straight your paths." By embracing God's supernatural patience, we allow God's guidance to steer our boat, helping us move forward on our life's journey unencumbered by the baggage of impatience.

Therefore, we do not think our way into righteousness. If we are learning to have patience as a virtue, that means it is not just us memorizing the Ten Commandments or Colossians. We rely on the Holy Spirit to develop our patience as a process.

Three qualities of patience:

1. **Self-control**: The ability to manage one's reactions and endure difficult situations without complaint.

2. **Humility**: Recognizing that we are no more important than others and accepting the need to wait.

3. **Generosity**: Smiling at the world even when faced with adversity, showing grace to others.

As I mentioned above, becoming patient and having patience as a virtue will not come by merely memorizing scripture. Do we need to have the Word of God stored in our hearts? Yes. Is memorizing scripture important? Of course. However, we don't develop our character by merely learning verses. Often, our character develops in our lives through the workings of the Holy Spirit. To be doers of the Word means, we must live by the Word of God and not just hearers.

Learning to be patient is like practicing a skill, such as playing a musical instrument. At first, it might seem hard, and we might not get it right away. Just as someone learning an instrument practices regularly to get better, developing patience involves practicing it regularly. It's about repeatedly choosing to stay calm and composed, especially when things don't go as planned. With time and practice, what was once difficult becomes more natural, and we find ourselves handling situations with patience more easily, much like a musician playing a piece smoothly after practicing it over and over.

Virtues are learned and acquired through practice and patience. The Bible provides guidance on cultivating patience through various practices.

Here are ten biblical principles and practices for developing patience:

1. **Prayer**: Philippians 4:6-7 encourages us to bring our concerns to God through prayer, trusting in His timing, and seeking His peace.

2. **Trusting God's Timing**: Ecclesiastes 3:1-8 reminds us that there is a time for everything, and trusting in God's timing requires patience.

3. **Counting Trials as Joy**: James 1:2-4 teaches that facing trials with joy leads to patience and spiritual maturity.

4. **Bearing with One Another**: Ephesians 4:2 urges believers

to bear with one another in love, demonstrating patience in relationships.

5. **Fruits of the Spirit**: Galatians 5:22-23 lists patience as one of the fruits of the Spirit, emphasizing its importance in a Citizen's life.

6. **Waiting on the Lord**: Psalm 27:14 encourages waiting patiently for the Lord and taking refuge in Him.

7. **Learning from Biblical Examples**: Romans 15:4 suggests that through the Scriptures, we can learn patience from the examples of those who endured challenges.

8. **Practicing Love**: 1 Corinthians 13:4 highlights that love is patient, emphasizing patience as a fundamental aspect of love.

9. **Endurance through Hope**: Romans 8:25 teaches that patience is tied to hope, and waiting with endurance is part of the citizen's journey.

10. **Seeking Wisdom**: Proverbs 19:11 advises that a person's wisdom yields patience, and it is to one's glory to overlook an offense.

By incorporating our helper, the Holy Spirit, and biblical principles into our daily lives, individuals can nurture a patient and Godly character, aligning their actions with the teachings found in the Scriptures. After practice, patience becomes a virtue. Patience becomes a virtue when it goes beyond just passive waiting and transforms into an active demonstration of faith, resilience, and trust in God's plan for our lives.

Biblical Examples of Patience and Perseverance

David, the anointed king of Israel, exemplifies supernatural patience. Anointed as a teenager, he didn't ascend to the throne until he was thirty—a fifteen-year wait filled with trials and tribulations. David faced numerous challenges, including evading King Saul, and dealing with his failings. Yet, he always turned back to God for forgiveness and strength (2 Samuel 22:7). God had a plan, and David learned that his trust had to be in God alone.

Job is another prime example of patience and endurance in the face of suffering. Despite losing his wealth, health, and family, Job remained steadfast in his faith and trusted in God's plan. His story teaches us that patience is not merely the act of waiting but maintaining faith and integrity even when life becomes overwhelmingly difficult. In James 5:11, Job is praised for his perseverance: "As you know, we count as blessed those who have persevered. You have heard of Job's perseverance and have seen what the Lord finally brought about. The Lord is full of compassion and mercy."

Jeremiah 29:11 tells us that while we plan our ways, it is God who directs our paths. We must exercise patience as He unfolds His divine plans for our lives, for we often cannot see the pitfalls that lie ahead. Trusting in God means walking by faith, knowing that He is orchestrating everything for our good.

Through the story of Job, we see that patience is not just about tolerating hardship but also about trusting in God's wisdom and timing. It's a virtue that involves faith, endurance, and a deep understanding that even amid trials, God's plan is greater than our immediate circumstances. David's patience stemmed from his deep trust in God. Your patience will flourish in the same way. God often tests our trust through circumstances designed to challenge us. When difficulties arise, they reveal where our trust truly lies.

Patience is not practiced in a vacuum; it emerges from our interactions with life's challenges. The depth of our patience correlates with our humility and our ability to trust God wholeheartedly.

To cultivate patience, immerse yourself in Psalm 37:4-5: "Delight yourself in the Lord, and He will give you the desires of your heart. Commit your way to the Lord; trust in Him, and He will act." Meditating on this scripture strengthens your resolve to find joy in the journey, even amidst trials. Real patience flourishes where spirituality resides. Our calling is to walk in the Spirit, allowing God's patience to blossom in our lives.

For those of us in Apostolic ministry—students of the Word and followers of Christ—patience becomes even more crucial. You will often find yourself on the front lines, facing challenges and hostilities directed at God's truth. This is where supernatural patience becomes essential, enabling you to enjoy the journey despite the hurdles.

James 1:2 reminds us to "count it all joy" when we face trials. Although weeping may endure for a night, joy indeed comes in the morning. Every challenge you face is a building block for your patience, allowing you to savor each moment.

Having joy in the Lord means celebrating God amidst your challenges. If you find yourself overwhelmed by frustration, you may miss the very assignment God has for you. You might be unable to hear the Holy Spirit prompting you to reach out to someone in need. Waiting on God is an active process. It's about working on your strategy, moving forward, and preparing for the promises God has for you. Faith is action. As you exercise your faith in patience, joy will naturally emerge.

Supernatural Patience Conclusion

Galatians 5:22-23 tells us that the fruit of the Spirit includes love, joy, peace, and patience. Remember, patience is not merely the ability to wait; it's how we act while waiting.

How do you conduct yourself as you await God's promises? Are you operating from a place of supernatural patience? Invite God to work within you, letting that patience rise to the surface, knowing that everything is in His capable hands.

As we deepen our relationship with Jesus, patience grows within us, flowing naturally from our connection to Him. John 15:4-5 says, "Abide in me, and I in you. As the branch cannot bear fruit by itself unless it abides in the vine, neither can you, unless you abide in me."

Growing in patience involves remembering God's faithfulness and trusting that He is working all things for the good of those who love Him

(Romans 8:28). By looking to biblical examples of endurance and relying on the Holy Spirit, we develop a character that reflects the patience of Christ in all situations.

Supernatural patience is about enduring trials and challenges with a steadfast heart. It's not about avoiding difficulties but facing them with resilience, wisdom, and faith. As we wait on the Lord, we develop spiritual maturity and learn to trust in His timing. Patience, in the biblical sense, is the art of thinking beyond the present moment and enduring with hope and perseverance.

Take a moment to affirm this: I am absorbing the nutrient of supernatural patience. Say it again.

In this journey of life, supernatural patience is a gift that allows you to savor each moment, trusting in God's perfect timing. As you develop this patience, you will find joy, peace, and fulfillment, walking confidently.

When patience is fully absorbed as a spiritual nutrient, it anchors you in God's love, keeping you strong and unmoved by circumstances while allowing you to extend that same love to others. It is a vital element in becoming rooted and grounded in God's love (Ephesians 3:17). Allow God's love to cultivate in you a steadfast, enduring, and long-suffering spirit, even in difficult or trying circumstances.

Author
Christian Andrew

Christian Andrew is a dynamic entrepreneur, brand strategist, and minister dedicated to helping others achieve success with purpose. As the founder of CXA Empire, he specializes in branding and image strategy, empowering individuals and businesses to elevate their presence and make a lasting impact.

With a passion for excellence and innovation, Christian has built a reputation for helping others refine their brand identity and messaging. He has had the opportunity to collaborate with leaders across various industries, including business, entertainment, politics, and faith, using his expertise to strengthen their brands and expand their reach. His keen eye for detail, strategic mindset, and ability to craft meaningful narratives make him a trusted voice in the industry.

Beyond business, Christian serves in ministry at the Kingdom Alliance of Churches International (KACI) and is committed to inspiring others through faith, mentorship, and personal growth. He believes in the power of perseverance and self-belief, using his journey to encourage others to pursue their dreams fearlessly. His work is rooted in integrity, service, and a deep commitment to uplifting others.

With a visionary mindset and an unwavering commitment to purpose, Christian Andrew continues to shape brands, inspire lives, and make a meaningful impact.

Chapter 2
THE NUTRIENT OF KINDNESS

"Love is kind."
(1 Corintians 13:4)

In the journey of spiritual growth, love serves as the fertile soil where we are called to be rooted and grounded. As trees of righteousness, we are meant to bear fruit, but this can only happen when the soil of our hearts is rich with the essential nutrients of God's love. One of these vital nutrients is kindness.

When we think of kindness, we might envision random acts of generosity or simple politeness. Yet, the biblical perspective of kindness digs much deeper. In 1 Corinthians 13:4, Paul writes, "Charity suffereth long, and is kind." This kindness is more than being nice; it is a divine attribute, powerful enough to transform lives and draw souls to repentance.

To understand the significance of kindness, we must first consider the metaphor of soil. Just as plants need nutrient-rich soil to grow, we need the rich soil of God's love to thrive spiritually. In gardening, soil provides nutrient absorption, water retention, root anchorage, gas exchange, and the presence of microorganisms essential for growth. Likewise, the soil of God's love supplies us with the nutrients needed for spiritual health, including patience, kindness, and more.

Nutrients do not remain idle in the soil; they are absorbed and circulated throughout the plant, ultimately contributing to the fruit it bears. In the same way, the nutrients of God's love—like kindness—must be absorbed

into our hearts, influencing our actions and interactions. It is not enough to receive kindness from God; we must actively demonstrate it to others.

The True Meaning of Kindness

A deeper exploration of the Greek language reveals the profound nature of kindness as intended in scripture. In 1 Corinthians, the word for "kind" is Chresteuomai, which means to show oneself mild or to be kind. This is a conjugated form of Chrestos, meaning suitable, well-fitted, useful, good, and benevolent. This is not passive kindness; it is active, eternally useful, and focused on the benefit of the recipient. It is kindness without the motive of personal gain.

This type of kindness transcends cultural norms of politeness or niceness. It is not merely about being friendly or considerate. It is about being good and eternally useful, acting with benevolence regardless of personal benefit. It is the kindness that seeks the well-being of others, rooted in love and designed to fulfill a purpose far beyond the momentary act.

Biblical kindness is not conditional; it is not reserved for those who can return the favor. It is meant to reach the lost, the broken, and the marginalized. It is for the young woman facing an unplanned pregnancy, the person struggling with addiction, or the individual wrestling with their identity just as much as it is for the saints. Our kindness should be like that of Christ, who loved and reached out to the least and the lost. This type of kindness does not judge or condemn; it draws people to God's love. If God's kindness led us to repentance, how much more should our kindness lead others to experience His love and grace?

Just as a plant absorbs nutrients from the soil, we must absorb the kindness of God's love and allow it to flow through us. It is not enough to receive kindness; we are called to demonstrate it, to grow strong and bear fruit that reflects His character. Ephesians 4:32 commands us to "be kind one to another, tenderhearted, forgiving one another, even as God for Christ's sake hath forgiven you."

This is where the challenge begins. It's easy to be superficially nice or polite, but to demonstrate biblical kindness requires us to be actively and intentionally benevolent. It demands that we love without seeking personal gain; It empowers us to be actively, eternally useful in the lives of others.

We must be kind to one another—not just in words, but in deeds. It means checking on the person who seems distant, praying for someone in need, and offering help without expecting anything in return. It requires us to look beyond surface-level and engage with others in ways that are good and beneficial for their growth and well-being.

In 1 Corinthians 13:4, Paul doesn't separate patience and kindness; he links them with "and." These two nutrients often work together. Just as some nutrients in soil are only effective when paired with others, our kindness must often be accompanied by patience. We may need to show kindness repeatedly before it bears fruit.

God has been endlessly patient and kind to us. He did not give up on us after one act of kindness. He continued to reach out to us, even when we were undeserving. In the same way, we are called to be patient in our kindness toward others.

True kindness involves stepping out of our comfort zones and engaging with people in meaningful ways. It means being present for someone in their time of need, lending a helping hand without expecting anything in return, or simply offering a listening ear. This type of kindness requires us to be sensitive to the needs of others and willing to respond, even when it is inconvenient.

Kindness is not always grand or dramatic. It can be found in the smallest gestures—a smile, a word of encouragement, or a helping hand. But what sets biblical kindness apart is its motivation. It is driven by love and a desire to be useful, not by the need for recognition or reward.

Our communities are filled with people in need of kindness. From the single mother struggling to make ends meet to the elderly neighbor who feels isolated, opportunities for kindness are all around us. But kindness is not merely about giving to those in need; it is about affirming the worth and dignity of every person.

Consider the young woman facing an unplanned pregnancy. She may feel alone, judged, and hopeless. Kindness might look like coming alongside her, offering support, listening without judgment, and helping her find resources. It is not about solving her problems for her but about empowering her with love and encouragement.

Think about the person struggling with addiction or mental health challenges. Kindness could involve being a consistent presence, offering compassion instead of condemnation, and reminding them of their value. It requires patience and a willingness to walk with them on their journey, no matter how long it takes.

Even within our churches, the need for authentic kindness is vast. We cannot be content with surface-level niceties or church clichés. We must engage with one another deeply, noticing when someone is struggling and being willing to help.

It is easy to say, "I'll pray for you," and then go about our day without giving it another thought. But biblical kindness requires action. It means following up, checking in, and being available to help however we can. Our churches must be places where people feel safe to share their burdens without fear of gossip or judgment. This requires us to be intentional in our kindness, creating an atmosphere of love, acceptance, and genuine care.

Biblical kindness is especially powerful when extended to those whom society marginalizes. It is for the person who feels unworthy, the outcast who has been shunned, and the sinner who thinks they are beyond redemption. Imagine the young man wrestling with his identity or the person struggling with addiction who walks into church, unsure if they belong. How do we respond? Do we look away, whisper, or judge? Or do we actively engage them with kindness?

Active kindness approaches these individuals with love and acceptance. It doesn't shy away from their struggles but walks alongside them. It offers hope, help, and healing. Just as Jesus reached out to the woman at the well, the tax collector, and the leper, we are called to reach out to those who are hurting and broken.

Kindness in Imperfect Places

One of the most radical aspects of biblical kindness is its refusal to judge. In a world quick to condemn, kindness seeks to understand and empathize. It meets people where they are without demanding that they first clean themselves up or meet certain standards.

Jesus demonstrated this beautifully when He encountered the woman caught in adultery. The religious leaders were ready to stone her, but Jesus responded with compassion and forgiveness. He showed her kindness without condoning her sin, offering her a path to redemption.

We are called to show this same kindness. It does not mean compromising our values or condoning wrongdoing. Instead, it means loving people even in their brokenness and pointing them to the redemptive power of Christ's love.

The nutrients of love are most needed in imperfect, dirty, and challenging situations. Kindness is most potent when extended to those who seem unworthy or undeserving. It is in the muck and mire of life that kindness becomes transformative.

Consider the soil—a substance many of us wouldn't even want on our hands. Yet, it is in this dirty, imperfect medium that growth occurs. Likewise, our kindness is most powerful when extended in difficult, messy situations. It is in these moments that we reflect God's love most clearly.

In Romans 2:4, Paul declares, "Or despisest thou the riches of his goodness and forbearance and longsuffering; not knowing that the goodness of God leadeth thee to repentance?" Some translations use "kindness" instead of "goodness." This reveals that God's kindness is eternally useful, leading us to repentance and transformation. It is not just a passive tolerance; it is an active, purposeful invitation to change. Biblical kindness is not random or aimless. It is purposeful and strategic, designed to draw people to Christ ensuring that our kindness points them to the One who first loved us.

When I reflect on my journey of faith, I see how the kindness of God reached me even in my lowest moments. It met me in the dirty, broken places—the muck and mire of my personal life. In those moments when I was hopeless and had nothing to offer, God was actively kind to me. His kindness was good and it was eternally useful, guiding me back to Him.

This is the nature of God's kindness: it reaches into the dirt, the imperfection, the brokenness, and offers love. It doesn't simply overlook our failures; it draws us to Him.

Jesus exemplified this type of kindness throughout His ministry. He was known for crossing social and cultural boundaries to show compassion and love. He touched lepers, ate with sinners, and engaged with the marginalized. His kindness was radical and transformative because it met people where they were and lifted them out of their circumstances.

If we are to follow Christ's example, our kindness must go beyond our comfort zones. It must reach out to people who are different from us, those who may be overlooked or even avoided by society. It means offering love and support to those who cannot repay us and standing beside people when it's inconvenient or uncomfortable.

The Eternal Impacts of Kindness

Kindness that is rooted in God's love does more than make someone's day better; it can change the trajectory of their life. It plants seeds of hope, healing, and faith. It opens doors for conversations about Christ and creates opportunities for people to experience God's love firsthand.

I remember hearing the story of a young man who visited a church, unsure of his faith and struggling with feelings of rejection. An older gentleman approached him with a warm smile, a firm handshake, and genuine interest in his life. That simple act of kindness changed everything for him. He felt seen, valued, and loved. It led him to give his life to Christ.

This is the power of kindness in action. It is not just about doing good deeds but about reflecting the heart of God. It is about loving people the way Christ loved us—actively and intentionally.

Conclusion: Our Call to Action

Our world is in desperate need of authentic, genuine kindness—kindness that is good, eternally useful, and motivated purely by love without selfish gain.

We are called to be vessels of God's kindness, bringing hope and healing to a broken world. Our kindness should cross boundaries, reach the marginalized, and transform lives. It should draw people to the love of Christ, just as His kindness drew us.

Let us be active agents of God's love, showing kindness in action—good, eternally useful, and selfless. Let us be rooted and grounded in the rich soil of God's love, bearing fruit that remains and reflects the character of Christ.

Author

Terry Henson

Terry Henson is an inspiring speaker, advocate for women and children, facilitator and confidante to ministry and community leaders. Terry's passion for serving the needs of women and families is evident through her ongoing work in the local community and her international mission's work which provides humanitarian relief for ongoing outreach projects in Kenya, Africa.

Terry is an accomplished entrepreneur, and along with her husband they own and operate Henson Properties, which provides tenant placement and property rehab services in and around Baltimore city. Terry is a retired federal employee and Civil Rights practitioner with over 25 years of experience as an Equal Employment Specialist.

She is a published author, trained mediator, certified end of life doula, conference facilitator and public speaker. Terry is a graduate of the American University Key Executive Leadership Certification Program and is the recipient of numerous awards and accolades.

Terry along with her husband Noland Henson pastored The New Life Church from 1993 to 2008, which served Anne Arundel County, Maryland with a primary focus of community outreach and evangelism. Currently Terry serves as an Associate Pastor at Kingdom Celebration Center in Gambrills, Maryland. She and her husband recently celebrated 43 years of marriage and are proudly dedicated to their family of 3 adult daughters and 4 grandchildren.

Chapter 3
THE NUTRIENT OF GENEROSITY

"Love does not seek her own"
(1 Corinthians 13:5)

Generosity is a virtue that reflects the heart of God and embodies the essence of love. As Christians, we are called to live lives deeply rooted in God's love, and generosity is one of the primary fruits that grow from that soil. It's more than an act of giving; it's a lifestyle of grace, kindness, and selflessness that seeks the highest good for others, much like the love of God toward humanity. Let's explore the biblical foundation of generosity, how it manifests in our lives, and why it is essential for cultivating a Christ-like existence.

Rooted in Love: The Foundation of Generosity

Generosity flows from a heart that is rooted in love, and this love is grounded in our relationship with God. Ephesians 3:14-20 (TLB) paints a beautiful picture of this foundation, describing the depth of God's love as something that surpasses all understanding. The passage encourages us to be "rooted and grounded in love" so that we can comprehend the vastness of God's love. This deep-rootedness allows us to give freely, just as God gives to us.

To be generous is to reflect God's own generosity, the ultimate expression of which is His sacrifice for us. John 3:16 reminds us that "God so loved the world that He gave His only begotten Son." This act of giving is the standard by which we measure our own generosity. Just as God did not withhold His best, we too are called to give our best in service to others, whether through material gifts, time, love, or care.

The Connection Between Love and Generosity

Jesus summarized the entirety of the Law in two commandments: love God and love your neighbor (Matthew 22:36-40). These commandments are intrinsically linked, as how we love our neighbor is a direct demonstration of how deeply we love God. Generosity is one of the clearest expressions of this love, revealing how much God's love has transformed our hearts.

In the Old Testament, two Hebrew words help us understand love: *"Chesed,"* which refers to God's faithful and committed love, and *"Ahavah,"* a love that is affectionate, caring, and active. The New Testament word *"Agape"* takes this even further, describing a love that seeks the highest good of another person without any expectation of personal gain. Agape love is at the heart of Christian generosity—it is selfless, abundant, and unconditional.

The Soil of God's Love: Nurturing Generosity

Just as plants require nutrients to grow, our spiritual lives need the right conditions to produce the fruit of generosity. The soil of God's love is rich with these nutrients, and one of the primary nutrients is generosity itself. Understanding the meaning of generosity is key: it is the spirit and action of freely and frequently giving to others, without expecting anything in return. It can take many forms—whether through acts of kindness, financial support, or simply offering one's time and attention to those in need.

God set the ultimate standard for generosity by giving His only Son as a sacrifice for our sins (Romans 5:6-8). This act of love and generosity bridged the gap between humanity and God, inviting us to respond by living generously ourselves. The love we receive from God is meant to be given away, not hoarded. We are designed to reproduce generosity in our lives, reflecting God's character to the world around us.

The Harmony of Generosity in Relationships

Generosity is not just about individual acts but also about cultivating harmonious relationships where generosity flows freely. Whether in marriage, friendship, or community, relationships require a constant exchange of generosity. This "Dance of Harmony," as I call it, is not about balance—because balance is rarely achieved—but about living in agreement and complementing one another.

Harmony in relationships creates an environment where generosity can thrive. Consider the example of an orchestra: individual musicians come together, each playing their own instrument, to create a symphony. The goal is harmony, not balance. Sometimes one instrument will dominate, and at other times, another will take the lead. Generosity allows this dynamic to function smoothly, as individuals make space for one another, offering what they have for the greater good.

Generosity in relationships, whether in a marriage or a family, often requires sacrifice, grace, and patience. It's about enriching each other's lives, not keeping score. This kind of generosity is a reflection of God's generous love toward us, and when we live generously in our relationships, we experience a taste of His divine harmony.

Generosity as a Reproductive Force

Everything that God creates is designed to reproduce, and generosity is no exception. Just as the earth brings forth life, generosity brings forth more generosity. Genesis 2:7 tells us that after God formed man from the dust of the earth, He breathed life into him. The first thing Adam did was breathe out the breath that God had given him. In this simple act, we see a profound truth: we are created to give away what God has given to us.

Generosity, like God's breath in Adam, is meant to be shared. It is a force that multiplies as it is practiced. When we live generously, we breathe life into the world around us. Our words, actions, and resources become instruments of God's grace, bringing His love to those who need it most. This is why we are called to be generous blessings—because we have been generously blessed.

The Triggers of Generosity

Generosity doesn't just happen by chance; it is cultivated by certain "triggers" that activate a generous spirit within us. These triggers include our words, humility, and compassion.

- **Words**: Our words have the power to build up or tear down. Proverbs 16:23-24 tells us that "pleasant words are like a honeycomb, sweet to the soul and healing to the bones." When we speak with kindness and encouragement, we open the door for generosity to flow. Our words can inspire others to be generous and can create a culture of generosity in our communities.

- **Humility**: Generosity requires humility, the willingness to think of others before ourselves. James 4:10 reminds us to "humble ourselves before the Lord," and in doing so, we allow God to lift us up. Humility makes room for generosity because it frees us from pride and self-centeredness, allowing us to see the needs of others and respond with compassion.

- **Compassion**: Compassion is the feeling that arises when we see someone suffering and feel motivated to relieve their suffering. In Genesis 45, we see Joseph, who despite being wronged by his brothers, responded with generosity and compassion when he had the power to punish them. Compassion moves us to act generously because it connects us to the pain and struggles of others.

By cultivating these triggers in our lives, we can create an environment where generosity flows naturally. Generosity becomes not just an occasional act but a way of life, rooted in God's love and sustained by His grace.

Generosity Beyond Material Gifts

It's important to remember that generosity is not limited to material gifts. In fact, it's an insult to God to reduce generosity to only monetary giving. True generosity encompasses much more—our time, our attention, our kindness, our wisdom, and our love. When we give generously, we reflect the goodness of God, who gives abundantly in all things, not just in material wealth.

Generosity, then, is a comprehensive way of living that touches every part of our lives. It's about being generous with our words, offering encouragement and support. It's about being generous with our time, giving our attention to those who need it. It's about being generous with our love, showing grace and compassion to those who are hurting. And yes, it's about being generous with our resources, using what God has given us to bless others.

Conclusion

Generosity is a reflection of God's heart, and a natural outcome of a life rooted in His love. It is not just a one-time act but a lifestyle that seeks to bless others in every possible way. As followers of Christ, we are called to cultivate generosity in the soil of God's love, allowing it to grow and reproduce in our lives.

Let us be generous in all things, knowing that we have been blessed to be a blessing. When we live generously, we reflect the love of God to the world, and in doing so, we fulfill our purpose as His ambassadors. Generosity is not only a gift we give to others; it is a gift that transforms us, bringing us closer to the heart of God and deeper into the harmony of His Kingdom.

Let me leave you with this extreme example of generosity demonstrated by a group of indigenous village children in western Africa.

Ubuntu (Zulu pronunciation: [ùbúntʼù])[1] (meaning *humanity* in Bantu) describes a set of closely related African-origin value systems that emphasize the <u>interconnectedness of individuals with their surrounding societal and physical worlds</u>. "Ubuntu" is sometimes translated as *"I am because we are"* (also "I am because you are"), or "humanity towards others" (Zulu *umuntu ngumuntu ngabantu*). In Xhosa, the latter term is used, but is often meant in a more philosophical sense to mean "the belief in <u>a universal bond of sharing that connects all humanity.</u>"

Legend has it that a western anthropologist visiting a village in Africa, to study the social behavior of an indigenous tribe. He proposed a game to a group of small children and they agreed to be a part of it. He placed a basket of fruit under a tree and asked the children to stand a few hundred feet away. "Whoever reaches the basket first gets all the treats and could eat it all by him or herself." He lined them all up and shouted "Ready, set, go!"

Something astonishing happened. The children took each other's hand and started running together. They all reached the basket at the same time, then they sat down in a big circle and enjoyed the fruits together, laughing and smiling the whole time. The anthropologist could not believe what he saw, and he asked them why they had waited for one another, as one could have taken the whole basket of fruit all for him or herself. The children shook their head and replied – **UBUNTU!** *How can one of us be happy if all the others are sad?*

One of the sayings in the country is **UBUNTU**. It means I AM BECAUSE WE ALL ARE! It is the essence of being human and demonstrating generosity.

---

1   Tutu, Desmond (2013). "Who we are: Human uniqueness and the African spirit of Ubuntu". YouTube. Archived from the original on 10 November 2021.

.

Author
Rhonda Sneed

Dr. Rhonda Sneed is the founder and CEO of Restoring Souls Outreach Center, INC., a nonprofit organization (501C3), and Lord Make Me Over Women's Conference in Houston, TX. Dr. Sneed is a Board-Certified Christian Counselor, Certified Anger Resolution Therapist, Certified Mental Health First Aider, Certified Christian Chaplain, Educator, Child Advocate, Ordained Pastor, Motivational & Inspirational Speaker, Model, and Author. She holds a Bachelor's Degree in Theology and Biblical Counseling, Master's in Educational Administration, and a PH.D in Christian Counseling and Psychology. Dr. Sneed's passion is to educate, equip and empower individuals with the necessary tools to live a productive and purpose-filled life. Dr. Sneed and her husband, Rodney, are the proud parents of three children, Jasmine, Raven and RJ, two son-in-laws Marion and Keshun, one daughter-in-law Kate and are grandparents to two beautiful girls, Peyton and Presley.

Chapter 4
THE NUTRIENT OF PEACE

"Love is not easily provoked."
(1 Corinthians 13:5)

What is Peace?

Peace is a state of tranquility, freedom from disturbance, and harmony in relationships. It is one of the attributes of God's love and a vital nutrient for spiritual growth. Like essential minerals that nourish a tree through its roots, peace sustains our spiritual lives, allowing us to withstand storms and bear fruit in all seasons.

In Hebrew, the word Shalom is translated as "peace." A closer look at *Shalom* reveals a more comprehensive definition of *wholeness in life through a right relationship with God, others, and creation.* Just as a tree requires multiple nutrients from rich soil to flourish, our souls require the complete nourishment that true peace—Shalom—provides.

This peace is not merely the absence of conflict but the presence of wholeness. It means finding rest and stillness in the heart despite challenges and striving to create an environment where all can thrive. This type of peace pushes through every disturbing circumstance that life can throw at you, enabling you to live a purposeful and productive lifestyle. As Jesus promised:

"I am leaving you with a gift—peace of mind and heart. And the peace I give is a gift the world cannot give. So don't be troubled or afraid." (John 14:27)

Just as a tree's roots must penetrate deeply into nutrient-rich soil, we must allow the peace of God to penetrate deeply into our hearts and minds. Before you can absorb the nutrient of peace, you must experience a transformation of your mind. In other words, you will need to change your way of thinking!

"Don't copy the behavior and customs of this world, but let God transform you into a new person by changing the way you think. Then you will learn to know God's will for you, which is good and pleasing and perfect." (Romans 12:2 NLT)

Peace: The Essential Nutrient for Spiritual Stability

Consider how trees with deep roots remain stable during powerful storms. Similarly, when peace is deeply rooted in our hearts, we remain steadfast when life's tempests rage around us. Peace allows us to respond rather than react when provoked.

Each day you are faced with choices. Every choice you make—words, thoughts, and actions—has the power to direct you toward peace or chaos. Just as a gardener carefully tends the soil around a young tree, we must tend to our inner life by making choices that foster peace.

"The tongue has the power of life and death, and those who love it will eat its fruit." (Proverbs 18:21 NIV)

When we speak words of peace, we create an environment where relationships can flourish. When we think thoughts aligned with God's truth, we cultivate inner tranquility that sustains us through difficulties. When our actions reflect the peaceful nature of Christ, we become like trees planted by rivers of water, whose leaves do not wither (Psalm 1:3).

- What choice will you make today to protect your peace?
- What choice will you make to deepen your relationship with God?

The choices you make today could determine your future. The choices you make demonstrate if you are absorbing the love nutrient of peace. Choose wisely and intentionally.

"Look! I stand at the door and knock. If you hear my voice and open the door, I will come in, and we will share a meal together as friends. Those who are victorious will sit with me on my throne, just as I was victorious and sat with my Father on his throne. Anyone with ears to hear must listen to the Spirit and understand what he is saying to the churches." (Revelation 3:20-22 NLT)

Change Is Required for Deeper Roots

Just as a tree's roots must sometimes break through rocky soil to reach water sources, our spiritual growth often requires breaking through resistance to change. Walking in peace demands self-discipline and commitment. Are you ready to embrace change, or will you continue to rely on your own understanding, refusing to seek and listen to God?

Absorbing the nutrient of peace necessitates change, which is often uncomfortable but essential. Change can take place with or without your permission. Change means moving in a new direction, and it can make you feel afraid and uncomfortable. We are often afraid because change can be out of our control, and we become unsure of what is in store for the future.

But when we strive to walk in peace, we can be assured our constant source of encouragement through this change process is the word of God, which is God speaking to us from a voice of love. Like a gardener's manual that guides the cultivation of a healthy tree, God's Word provides direction for nurturing peace in our lives.

Why do we resist change?

- Lack of knowledge: Without understanding the benefits of peace, we may resist the changes required to cultivate it.
- Lack of wisdom: We may fail to see how current behaviors disrupt our peace.
- Lack of faith: We may doubt God's ability to sustain us through change.

- Lack of trust: We may question whether God's way is truly better than our own.
- Pride: We may think our way is superior.
- Stubbornness: We may simply refuse to yield to God's direction.
- Disobedience: We may knowingly reject God's commands.

In times of change, we usually become fearful or anxious because we're not sure of what is going to happen or how everything will unfold. The unknown, the unfamiliar, can be intimidating. But you must rest in the truth, knowing that God has a plan for you and will lead you on the right path when you place your trust in Him. Like a strong tree that bends with the wind without breaking, we can remain flexible yet firmly rooted in God's promises.

> *"For I know the plans I have for you," says the Lord. "They are plans for good (Shalom) and not for disaster, to give you a future and a hope."* (Jeremiah 29:11 NLT, parenthesis added)

When you enter a season of change, your mind can become crowded with questions that weigh you down or a never-ending to-do list that entangles you in the tiny details, causing you to grow weary and tired. When faced with change, trust in God's plan. Clear your mind, stay flexible, and remain focused on Him. This will allow you to have faith and believe that your changes will benefit your ability to absorb the nutrient of peace and apply it to your daily living.

> *"Don't be afraid, for I am with you. Don't be discouraged, for I am your God. I will strengthen you and help you. I will hold you up with my victorious right hand."* (Isaiah 41:10 NLT)

When you walk in peace, you choose to accept change, trusting and obeying the process. You know that God loves you and has full control of your life. He will grant you renewed strength for this journey called life. There isn't anything like experiencing God's love, especially when He gives you peace amid chaotic circumstances and difficult relationships.

Spiritual Growth: A Lifelong Process of Nutrient Absorption

Just as a tree continues to grow throughout its lifetime, constantly drawing nutrients from the soil, spiritual growth is a lifelong process. It does not happen automatically. It is a conscious, ongoing journey of aligning your life with God's will and bettering yourself by learning to live a life that is pleasing to God using the fruits of the Spirit and gifts He has placed inside of you.

The more you grow spiritually, the more you choose to hear and obey God's voice and accept that obedience to God's word nurtures growth, while disobedience stunts it. Consider how a tree deprived of essential nutrients becomes weak, susceptible to disease, and fails to bear fruit. Similarly, when we neglect to absorb the nutrient of peace, our spiritual lives become vulnerable, and we struggle to demonstrate love that "is not easily provoked."

> *"The seeds that fell among the thorns represent those who hear the message, but all too quickly the message is crowded out by the cares and riches and pleasures of this life. And so, they never grow into maturity."* (Luke 8:14-15 NLT)

I firmly believe that before you can accomplish anything, you must have a plan of action. So, to walk in peace, you will have to be intentional and begin operating with a Growth Mindset!

Growth is the process of developing or maturing physically, mentally, or spiritually. Growth encompasses various aspects, including spiritual development, faith and knowledge, perseverance through trials, and bearing fruit in our lives.

Mindset means the established set of attitudes held by someone. A growth mindset is transformational. Transformation is when you make a thorough or dramatic change in form, appearance, or character (in this case, we refer to change in character).

Cultivating a Growth Mindset for Peace

Let's look at what a person does if they have the faith to transform their thinking process and adopt a Growth Mindset:

- Acknowledge God's authority over your life: Recognize that the Master Gardener knows what is best for your growth.
- Let go of fear, guilt, shame, and the opinions of others: Remove these toxic elements that contaminate the soil of your heart.
- Forgive yourself and others: Clear away the debris that prevents roots from growing deep.
- Be a good steward of your blessings: Use resources wisely to nourish continued growth.
- Express gratitude in all circumstances: Appreciate even the rain that helps you grow stronger.
- Reflect and take self-inventory on your actions: Regularly examine the health of your spiritual roots.
- Embrace mistakes as opportunities to gain experience: Learn from every season, even those that seem unfruitful.
- Recognize that you are not always right: Be open to correction that promotes better growth.
- Be quick to listen and slow to speak: Absorb wisdom before responding.
- Use wisdom in everything you do, and be intentional about the choices you make, and accept what God allows!: Trust the Gardener's plan for your life.

When you choose to operate in a growth mindset and walk in spiritual maturity and peace, you intentionally exercise your faith and focus on God's will for your life. Like a tree that naturally turns its leaves toward the sun, you orient your heart toward God's light and love.

"Then Joshua told the people, "Purify yourselves, for tomorrow the Lord will do great wonders among you." (Joshua 3:5)

It is time to declare today that I refuse to let anything or anybody, including myself, stop my Spiritual Growth process. I choose to operate in FAITH!

Focus

Activates

Intentional

Trust and yields a

Harvest

The Rich Soil of Emotional Intelligence

Peace and love are deeply interconnected with emotional intelligence (EI) because they influence how we understand, manage, and express emotions in a way that aligns with God's character. Emotional intelligence, at its core, is the ability to recognize and regulate our own emotions while also responding to others with wisdom and compassion.

When we cultivate peace and love, we enhance our emotional intelligence and build healthier relationships. Just as rich soil contains various minerals and nutrients that work together to nourish a tree, emotional intelligence combines several components that help us absorb and express God's peace:

1. Self-awareness: Recognizing our emotions and their impact on thoughts and behavior
2. Self-regulation: Managing disruptive emotions and impulses effectively
3. Motivation: Being driven by internal values rather than external rewards
4. Empathy: Understanding the emotional makeup of others
5. Social skills: Building rapport and managing relationships effectively

Love is not easily provoked (1 Corinthians 13:5). The more we absorb the nutrient of peace, the more we are less likely to fly off the handle with people. Peace stabilizes our emotions and grounds our thoughts to respond in a way that will benefit and not destroy our relationships with others. The love of God controls impulses and responds rather than react.

When we love others, we are sensitive to their emotions and perspectives, fostering deeper connections.

Like a mature tree that provides shade and shelter for others, emotional intelligence enables us to communicate effectively, resolve conflicts, and build trust in relationships. We become a source of refreshment and stability for those around us.

The peace of God causes us to become more aware of our emotions so that we can respond in love rather than out of hurt, anger, or frustration. It governs our actions. By seeking to understand others' emotions, we show love and create a safe haven for healthy conversations.

We should all dig our spiritual roots deep in the rich soil of God's love to absorb the nutrient of peace because it develops relational wisdom. We can grow to a place of maturity where our relationships will become more lasting and beneficial. You will be an asset to any relationship you experience. People will love to lodge around you because they will sense the love, calmness, and settledness exuding from your innermost being.

Peace in Desperate Times: Pushing Through to Purpose

How desperate are you to protect your peace and fulfill your God-given purpose? Living out your God-given purpose requires determination and endurance. Just as a tree in drought must extend its roots even deeper to find water, we sometimes must push through challenging circumstances to maintain our peace.

Consider the woman with the issue of blood in the book of Luke:

> *"Now a woman, having a flow of blood for twelve years, who had spent all her livelihood on physicians and could not be healed by any, came from behind and touched the border of His garment. And immediately her flow of blood stopped. And Jesus said, "Who touched Me?" When all denied it, Peter and those with him said, "Master, the multitudes throng and press You, and You say, 'Who touched Me?" But Jesus said, "Somebody touched Me, for I perceived power going out from Me." Now when the woman saw that she was*

not hidden, she came trembling; and falling down before Him, she declared to Him in the presence of all the people the reason she had touched Him and how she was healed immediately. And He said to her, "Daughter, be of good cheer; your faith has made you well. Go in peace." (Luke 8:43-48 NKJV)

Did she have to crawl? Yes...desperate times require desperate measures. Her crawling was a sign of her humility, unwavering faith, and desperation to be healed. Are you willing to do whatever it takes to be healed physically, spiritually, mentally, emotionally, and financially, so that you can experience the fullness of walking in peace and pursuing your purpose?

God's purpose for your life will always prevail:

"But indeed for this purpose I have raised you up, that I may show My power in you, and that My name may be declared in all the earth." (Exodus 9:16 NKJV)

"You can make many plans, but the Lord's purpose will prevail." (Proverbs 19:21 NLT)

It is time to learn how to enjoy the process of discovering, uncovering, and recovering your purpose. Like a tree that fulfills its purpose by providing shade, fruit, oxygen, and beauty, you have a unique purpose in God's garden. When you absorb the nutrient of peace, you can fulfill this purpose even amid life's challenges.

Practical Ways to Absorb the Nutrient of Peace

Just as a gardener takes specific actions to ensure a tree receives proper nutrients, we can take practical steps to absorb more of God's peace:

- Ask God for wisdom and knowledge daily: Request the ability to recognize and apply peace in every situation.
- Practice fasting, prayer, and solitude: Create space to commune deeply with the Prince of Peace.
- Engage in service and worship: Express love outwardly as a natural outflow of inner peace.

- Fellowship with others striving to live Christ-like lives: Draw strength from the forest rather than standing alone.
- Study, meditate and journal on God's word daily: Absorb truth that nourishes peaceful living.
- Be mindful of what you feed into your spirit: Guard against influences that poison your peace.
- Train your thoughts: Direct your mind toward what is true, noble, right, pure, lovely, and admirable (Philippians 4:8).
- Create an attitude of gratitude and thanksgiving: Recognize God's provision in all circumstances.
- Set realistic goals and evaluate progress regularly: Monitor your growth in peace just as you would measure a tree's height.
- Prioritize self-care and enjoy life: Remember that even the strongest trees require rest and rejuvenation.
- Reposition yourself: Sometimes growth requires moving away from toxic environments into healthier soil.
- Learn how to laugh and enjoy life: Experience the fullness of joy that comes from a peaceful heart.

The Five C's to Protect Your Peace

Just as a gardener might install a fence around a newly planted tree, we need protective measures to guard our peace:

1. Commitment:

"Commit your actions to the Lord, and your plans will succeed." (Proverbs 16:3 NLT)

Make an unwavering decision to prioritize peace in your life.

2. Consistency:

"So let's not get tired of doing what is good. At just the right time we will reap a harvest of blessing if we don't give up." (Galatians 6:9 NLT)

Regularly nurture the soil of your heart with practices that promote peace.

3. Courage:

"Even when I walk through the darkest valley, I will not be afraid, for you are close beside me." (Psalms 23:4 NLT)

Face fears and challenges with the confidence that God's peace sustains you.

4. Clarity:

"The Lord directs the steps of the godly. He delights in every detail of their lives." (Psalms 37:23 NLT)

Maintain a clear vision of God's purpose for your life, allowing peace to guide your decisions.

5. Conviction:

"Blessed are those who don't feel guilty for doing something they have decided is right." (Romans 14:22 NLT)

Stand firmly in your commitment to peace, even when others choose conflict.

Peace as a Spiritual Legacy

Just as mature trees produce seeds that grow into new trees, your peace can multiply and bless generations to come. When we absorb the nutrient of peace and let it transform us, we become like those described in Isaiah 61:3—"oaks of righteousness, a planting of the LORD for the display of his splendor."

The peace we cultivate becomes a legacy that benefits not only us but those around us and those who come after us. Like a mighty oak that provides shelter for countless creatures and drops thousands of acorns that can grow into new trees, our peace can impact countless lives.

Reflect and Act

We are all created on purpose, with purpose, for purpose. How will you demonstrate God's love and share His peace with others? How will you ensure that your roots grow deep into the rich soil of God's love, absorbing the essential nutrient of peace?

"Write my answer plainly on tablets, so that a runner can carry the correct message to others. This vision is for a future time. It describes the end, and it will be fulfilled. If it seems slow in coming, wait patiently, for it will surely take place. It will not be delayed." (Habakkuk 2:2-3 NLT)

Are you ready for your life to yield a harvest? If so, let us move forward with commitment, courage, and a clear vision, while absorbing the love nutrient of peace. It is transformative, developing our minds, stabilizing our emotions, and encouraging us to make healthy choices that will benefit our lives and those we are in relationship with.

Let us protect our peace so that we can demonstrate the love of Christ and fulfill God's purpose for our lives. Like trees planted by rivers of water, we can grow strong, stable, and fruitful when our roots absorb the vital nutrient of peace from the rich soil of God's love.

Authors
Dominic & Rhoda Kudawoo

Pastor Dominic and Lady Rhoda Kudawoo are a dynamic, faith-driven couple committed to spreading God's love and serving their community. As the Senior Pastor and First Lady of House of Joy Global Ministries in Laytonsville, Maryland, they work side by side in shepherding a vibrant congregation. Pastor Dominic, a man of integrity and passion, has been dedicated to ministry for many years, delivering powerful teachings that connect biblical truths to everyday life. His heart for prayer, deliverance, and healing has left a lasting impact on countless individuals. A devoted husband and father of six, he is also passionate about providing pastoral care and counseling to families in need.

Lady Rhoda, a woman of vision and purpose, stands alongside her husband, offering her wisdom and support, especially in the areas of marriage counseling. With a special mandate for empowering women and couples, she inspires and uplifts through her teachings and conferences. As the founder and CEO of The Rhoyal Collection, a modest fashion brand, Lady Rhoda blends creativity with faith, encouraging individuals to embrace their royal identity in Christ.

Together, Pastor Dominic and Lady Rhoda exemplify servant leadership, grace, and resilience. Their combined commitment to faith, family, and community continues to make a lasting impact, and they remain dedicated to empowering others to live out their God-given purpose.

Chapter 5

THE NUTRIENT OF FORGIVENESS

"Love does not keep record of wrong."
1 Corinthians 13:5

One of the most remarkable tales I've come across regarding forgiveness goes something like this: *Once there was a man who carried a sack of stones everywhere he went. Each time someone hurt him, he added another stone. Over time, the sack became heavier, and his journey became exhausting. One day, he realized that the weight he carried wasn't punishing those who wronged him; it was only slowing him down. So, he began to forgive, tossing the stones away one by one. With each release, his steps grew lighter, and he discovered the joy of walking freely again. He learnt that forgiveness wasn't for others—it was for himself.*

Forgiveness is one of the most profound expressions of love, yet it can also be one of the toughest challenges we face. Although we often hear the term, it is much easier to preach than practice. Forgiveness goes beyond merely being a nice action or an act of letting go; it's a journey that often demands strength, reflection, humility, and time. At its essence, forgiveness is not solely about absolving others from their wrongdoings but rather about liberating oneself from the burden of pain and resentment.

The love described in the book of 1 Corinthians 13 invites us to strive for a higher standard, one that is rooted in God's essence. This scripture subtly addresses forgiveness through its focus on the attributes of love. Verse 5 is especially pertinent; it states that *"love does not keep a record of wrong"* (NIV) or *"thinks no evil"* (NKJV). This declaration challenges our natural instincts and encourages us to engage in the transformative process of forgiveness. This form of love is not merely a sentiment; it requires a conscious decision to forgive the offender and to entrust the offense to God.

Forgiveness often differs from our common perception; the Merriam-Webster Dictionary defines it as "relief from the guilt or penalty of an offense." However, a more comprehensive understanding of forgiveness is that it is a purposeful choice to let go of resentment, anger, or the desire for revenge against someone who has wronged or hurt you, regardless of whether they deserve it or seek reconciliation. It involves releasing negative feelings and opting to move forward without allowing the offense to dictate your emotions or actions.

In the biblical context, one of the Hebrew words for forgiveness is *"Selichah,"* which embodies grace and reflects God's mercy and love. As stated in Ephesians 4:32, forgiveness serves as both a divine gift and a directive to forgive others as we have been forgiven by God. Forgiveness does not necessarily entail forgetting or justifying the wrongdoing; rather, it liberates the forgiver from the shackles of bitterness and paves the way for healing.

In this chapter, we will explore the nature of forgiveness through the lens of God's love. We will discuss why forgiveness is an essential aspect of a life anchored in Christ and how we can actively implement this command. You'll discover that forgiveness isn't solely for the benefit of those who have harmed you; it's a transformative gift for your own heart that draws you closer to God's love. Let's embark on this journey together, learning to forgive as Christ forgave us, and becoming firmly rooted in the love that does not cling to past wrongs.

Why We Must Forgive

Why is forgiveness so vital? Is it necessary for me to forgive?

Forgiveness has always been at the heart of the Christian faith. It is grounded in the teachings of Jesus, and it exemplifies God's grace toward humanity. In fact, the bible not only encourages forgiveness but also commands it. The well-known English poet Alexander Pope once stated, *"To err is human, to forgive is divine,"* reminding us that making mistakes is a common part of being human, but forgiveness can be achieved through the help of God. Thus, forgiveness challenges us to overcome our shortcomings and reflect God's grace and mercy. The scriptures offer numerous instances of God's compassion towards us. It was His love that motivated Him to forgive us even when we least deserved it. Now, as His children we are called to embody that same love. By forgiving others, we reflect His character and exhibit His love in action (Psalm 103:8-10). Apostle Paul describes love as patient and kind, and does not keep records of wrong, emphasizing that forgiveness is an expression of love that originates from a heart filled with genuine Christ-like love.

In the book of Matthew 6:14-15, Jesus teaches that our ability to forgive others is directly connected to God's forgiveness of our sins. This highlights the importance of practicing forgiveness in our relationship with Him. Jesus demonstrated the ultimate act of forgiveness on the cross, when He prayed for those crucifying Him, saying "father forgive them for they do not know what they are doing." (Luke 23:24). How many of us can confidently say that we pray for those who wrong us? Yet, as followers of Christ, we are called to follow His example by forgiving even in the face of great wrongs. We must always remember that **OUR GOD IS A FORGIVING GOD!**

Moreover, forgiveness acknowledges our shared humanity; we are all flawed and in need of God's mercy. When we forgive, we recognize our own forgiveness. Although forgiveness can be challenging, it is an act of obedience to God's word. It takes faith to trust that God will execute justice in His own perfect way, as stated in Romans 12:9, *"Do not take revenge, my dear friends, but leave room for God's wrath, for it is written: it is mine to avenge; I will repay; says the Lord."* This helps us to release the need for retaliation or judgement. Ultimately, forgiveness is not optional in our faith but a crucial command. It is a practical means of living out the Gospel and aligning our hearts with God's will. Forgiveness encourages us to trust God's justice, accept His mercy, and share His grace with others.

The Bible instructs us to forgive everyone who wrongs us—**EVERYONE MEANS EVERYONE, INCLUDING YOURSELF.** God's message is straightforward: we are to offer forgiveness to all. No matter the severity of the offense or the nature of the relationship, whether it is a family member, friend, loved one, someone in the church, a stranger, an acquaintance, or even an unbeliever. Furthermore, the bible offers a clear yet challenging perspective on how often we must forgive. In Matthew 18:21-22, Peter asks Jesus, *"Lord, how many times shall I forgive my brother or sister who has sinned against me? Up to seven times? Jesus responds, "I tell you, not seven times, but seventy-seven times."* This response isn't about counting a specific number of offenses; it's about cultivating a heart of forgiveness. By using such an exaggerated figure Jesus emphasizes that forgiveness has no limit. Just as God's forgiveness towards us is infinite and unending, we are called to extend that same boundless grace to others.

How to Forgive

Forgiveness is an incredibly powerful means of achieving emotional and spiritual healing, yet it can also be one of the most challenging actions to undertake. When we experience hurt, betrayal, or wrongdoing, it's instinctive to cling to that pain as a defense mechanism or a way to seek retribution. However, we often fail to recognize that holding onto unforgiveness ultimately harms us more than the individual who caused the pain. Unforgiveness is a trap that can easily lead us into sin. It acts like a heavy burden that weighs down on our heart, mind, body, and it makes it challenging to live wholly and freely. An insightful saying describes unforgiveness as akin to drinking poison while expecting the other person to suffer. Therefore, it's crucial to rid ourselves of the toxic poison of unforgiveness.

In reality, forgiveness might not always be as straightforward as we would like it to be. Nevertheless, as believers we are called to forgive - not because it is easy, but because it is vital for our spiritual development and liberation. If you find it difficult to forgive, know that you are not alone. The encouraging news is that you don't have to navigate this process alone. God supplies both the guidance, and the strength needed for forgiveness. He equips us with practical steps to make forgiveness achievable. Let's discuss how to take that initial step, trusting God for the rest.

- Acknowledging the Hurt: Forgiveness starts with recognizing the pain from the hurt, betrayal or wrongdoing. It's not about denying the hurt but confronting it sincerely in God's presence. You must trust Him to heal your heart by spending more time in prayer regarding the situation. (Psalm 147:3)

- Pray for Strength: Through prayer and meditation on the Word of God, ask the Holy Spirit to soften your heart, remove any resentment and grant you the grace to let go (Philippians 4:13). Seek strength to release the offense and consciously decide to forgive, even when it feels challenging.

- Reflect on God's Forgiveness: Take a moment to think about how much God has forgiven you (Matthew 18:21-35). Recognizing His mercy towards you should motivate you to extend the same mercy to others.

- Decide to Release the Offense & Offender: Forgiveness is a choice, not merely a feeling. Make a deliberate decision to release the offense and the offender from the debt they owe you, placing them in God's hands for justice and mercy (Romans 12:19).

- Bless Don't Curse: In Luke 6:28, Jesus instructs us to pray for those who have wronged us. Pray for the individual who hurt you, asking God to work positively in their life. This will help change your perspective and align your heart with His will.

- Pursue Reconciliation When Appropriate: While forgiveness does not always entail restoring a close relationship, it does involve being open to reconciliation when suitable. Allow God's wisdom to guide your interactions.

- <u>Seek Counsel</u>: Seeking guidance can help you approach forgiveness wisely, with support from a pastoral team, professional counselors, and/or therapy (Proverbs 11:14).

- <u>Practice Daily Love</u>: Forgiveness is not just a one-time decision but a way of life. As 1 Corinthians 13:7 reminds us, love "always protects, always trusts, always hopes, always perseveres." Continually walk in God's love, letting it flow through you to others.

The Bottom Line

Forgiveness is not a quick or simple act; it is a journey that demands time and effort. It involves facing our pain, recognizing our feelings, and making a deliberate choice to let go of the bitterness and resentment we may be clinging to. When we opt for forgiveness, we align ourselves with God's intentions and reflect His grace and mercy to others, just as He has shown us. This act of obedience draws us nearer to His heart and allows us to enjoy the profound peace that comes from shedding our burdens and moving past our experiences. Through intentional and practical actions forgiveness evolves from merely a single instance into a transformative path that guides us towards emotional healing and spiritual development.

Always keep in mind the words of Jesus in Colossians 3:13 (ERV) "Don't be angry with each other but forgive each other. If you feel someone has wronged you, forgive them. Forgive others because the Lord forgave you"

A Prayer for You

Heavenly Father, we come before You today with hearts weighed down by pain, anger, and the burden of unforgiveness. You know the hurt we feel and the struggles we face as we try to let go of the offenses against us. Lord, we confess that we cannot do this with our own strength. We need Your grace, your love, and Your Spirit to guide us through this process.

Father, Your Word teaches that forgiveness is a reflection of Your love for us. You forgave us even when we didn't deserve it, and You sent Your Son, Jesus, to pay the ultimate price for our sins. Help us to grasp the depth of that love, so that we may extend it to others, even to those who have hurt us deeply.

Lord, we ask for healing where there has been wounding, peace where there has been turmoil, and understanding where there has been anger. Help us to release the offenses and give them to You, trusting that You are the righteous Judge who sees and knows all. Teach us, O God, to see the people who have hurt us through Your eyes—not excusing the wrong, but acknowledging that they, too, are in need of Your grace. Let our hearts be softened and renewed by Your Spirit, that we may walk in freedom, no longer bound by bitterness or resentment.

Thank You, Lord, for the freedom and joy that come through forgiveness. Strengthen us to take each step, no matter how small, toward this healing journey. May Your love flow through us and bring restoration, peace, and hope to our hearts and our relationships.

In Jesus' name, we pray, Amen.

Author
Aaron Montague

Aaron M. Montague, MDIV; MBA, is a retired veteran of the US Armed Forces, a life coach, and a Bible educator. He holds certification as a Veterans Appeals advocate with a nationally recognized Veterans Service Organization, bringing 25 years of experience to his role. With a distinctive combination of skills in hypno-trance therapy, NLP, and spiritual mentorship, Aaron is dedicated to empowering individuals, particularly veterans, to face life's changes with strength and intention. His transition from military life to becoming a supportive mentor and advocate illustrates his commitment to fostering both personal development and community enhancement. This book embodies his enduring mission to motivate others to pursue healing, faith, and personal advancement.

Chapter 6
THE NUTRIENT OF INTEGRITY

"Love rejoices with the truth."
1 Corinthians 13:5

Just as a tree thrives when planted in rich, fertile soil, our spiritual lives flourish when deeply rooted in the love of God. Integrity, like a vital nutrient in this divine soil, nourishes our faith, strengthens our character, and sustains our walk with Christ. Without integrity, our spiritual foundation weakens, leaving us vulnerable to deception, compromise, and instability. The purpose of this chapter is to explore integrity as an essential element in a believer's life, firmly grounded in the steadfast love of God. Integrity is not just about honesty but about wholeness—living in alignment with the truth and love of God in all areas of life.

The Soil of God's Love

The foundation of our spiritual growth is God's love, described beautifully in 1 Corinthians 13:4-8: "Love is patient, love is kind. It does not envy, it does not boast, it is not proud... Love never fails." Integrity is inseparably tied to this love because true integrity aligns our hearts with God's truth. When we embrace love as the foundation of our actions, our integrity becomes an outflow of that love. Without love, integrity becomes rigid legalism, but when cultivated in love, it produces life and authenticity.

A tree draws its sustenance from the soil, and the deeper its roots go, the stronger and more fruitful it becomes. Likewise, when we immerse ourselves in the love of God, our integrity is strengthened, enabling us to bear righteous fruit. The deeper our roots in God's love, the more resistant we are to the winds of temptation and the storms of adversity.

The Essence of Singleness

A tree with a deep and singular root system is stable. In the same way, integrity thrives when we have a singleness of heart, vision, purpose, and passion. James 1:8 warns against being "double-minded", emphasizing that a divided heart leads to instability. Singleness of heart means aligning every part of our being—our desires, motives, and actions—with God's will. When we live with this kind of integrity, our choices remain unwavering, guided by an undivided devotion to God's truth.

"Singleness of heart" represents a dedication that embodies genuine "integrity." It signifies living with a clear, cohesive "vision" for our lives—a "purpose" that inspires us and a "passion" that energizes us. This approach does not allow for "duplicity. Singleness of heart eliminates hypocrisy. It creates a consistency that runs through every aspect of our lives—our speech, our relationships, our decisions. It means we are the same in private as we are in public, that our inner thoughts match our outward expressions, and that our faith is evident in our conduct.

"Singleness of thought" enables us to concentrate on what truly matters, resulting in a life rich with "purpose and direction."

In "Singleness of vision," we connect with our deepest values. When we opt to perceive life through a transparent lens—one unclouded by fear or dishonesty—we uncover the beauty in every interaction, every choice, and every moment. "Singleness of vision" encourages us to honor our commitments, not out of obligation, but because it resonates with the truth of our being.

Integrity and the Root System of Faith

The deeper a tree's roots go, the more resistant it is to external forces. Likewise, our faith must be deeply rooted in integrity, keeping us firm when trials come. Proverbs 10:9 states, "Whoever walks in integrity walks securely, but he who makes his ways crooked will be found out." Integrity provides security because it removes the need for pretense. A believer grounded in integrity does not sway under pressure but remains steadfast, knowing their life is anchored in God's truth.

Integrity allows us to walk in peace. When we live truthfully, we do not have to worry about keeping up appearances or remembering falsehoods. We can stand before God and people with a clear conscience, confident that our character is sound. This security strengthens our faith, making us unshakable in times of difficulty.

The Dangers of Duplicity

A tree with a split root system will eventually weaken and die. Likewise, when we live with duplicity—presenting one face to the world while hiding another—we compromise our spiritual foundation. Duplicity breeds dishonesty, hypocrisy, and instability. Paul reminds us in 1 Corinthians 13 that love "does not delight in evil but rejoices with the truth." Integrity demands that we choose truth over deception, consistency over convenience, and authenticity over appearance.

Duplicity divides the soul, creating conflict between what we profess and how we actually live. Jesus condemned duplicity in the Pharisees, calling them "whitewashed tombs" (Matthew 23:27)—outwardly appearing righteous but inwardly full of corruption. The warning is clear: integrity is not about maintaining an image but about embodying truth.

Living with duplicity means wearing a mask in public while concealing ulterior motives, which can lead to a fractured identity. It can also make us two-faced individuals, behaving one way in front of others while secretly nurturing different intentions. In 1 Corinthians 13, Paul states that love "is not self-seeking." Duplicity thrives on selfishness, pushing us to manipulate, to say one thing while doing another, and to prioritize appearances over genuine authenticity.

Integrity and duplicity are fundamentally incompatible concepts that represent opposing forces in human relationships and interactions.

Integrity is rooted in honesty, transparency, and a steadfast commitment to the truth. It is the quality that enables individuals to be reliable and trustworthy, fostering an environment where genuine connections can thrive. When people act with integrity, they establish a foundation of trust and loyalty, which are essential for healthy relationships, whether personal or professional.

On the other hand, duplicity thrives on deception and falsehoods. It is characterized by a lack of consistency between one's words and actions, often leading to manipulation and betrayal. Duplicity undermines the very fabric of relationships, breeding suspicion and doubt. When individuals engage in duplicitous behavior, they create a chasm between what they say and what they do, leading to confusion and emotional turmoil for those on the receiving end.

integrity and duplicity are at odds with one another, each shaping the dynamics of relationships in profoundly different ways. Integrity nurtures trust, loyalty, and genuine connection, while duplicity sows discord, suspicion, and emotional pain. The choice between these two paths ultimately determines the quality and depth of our relationships, underscoring the vital importance of honesty and authenticity in our interactions with others.

Multiplicity – The Distracted Heart

Another threat to integrity is multiplicity—being pulled in multiple directions, making it difficult to stay committed to a single purpose. When we lack focus, we drift aimlessly, vulnerable to worldly influences. Paul's reminder that love "always perseveres" encourages us to resist distractions and remain faithful. Integrity calls for a focused heart—one that remains unwavering in its devotion to Christ, despite the world's ever-changing priorities.

When we allow distractions to take root, our spiritual growth is hindered. Like weeds that choke a healthy plant, multiple conflicting desires can drain our strength and prevent us from flourishing. Integrity requires an undivided heart, fixed on Christ and His kingdom.

Passion and Purpose Anchored in Integrity

Our purpose and passion must be firmly rooted in integrity. A person of integrity does not chase fleeting desires but remains faithful to God's calling. Proverbs 11:3 states, "The integrity of the upright guides them." This guidance keeps us aligned with truth, enabling us to walk confidently in our purpose without fear of shifting external pressures. Passion that flows from integrity is enduring and resilient, sustaining us through challenges and trials.

When our passion is driven by integrity, it is not easily extinguished. It fuels perseverance, giving us the strength to endure hardships and remain steadfast in our faith. True passion is not momentary excitement but a deep, abiding commitment to righteousness.

The Benefits of Integrity

Embracing integrity is not just a personal choice; it is a transformative journey that cultivates a deep sense of tranquility within us and strengthens our relationships with others. When we live with integrity, we remove the internal struggles that often arise from dishonesty or hidden motives. There is no discord in our hearts, no gnawing remorse from concealed actions or ulterior agendas. Instead, we free ourselves from the pressure of upholding facades, allowing our lives to align naturally with our core values. This freedom creates fertile ground for joy, connection, and authentic relationships to thrive.

Integrity serves as a strong foundation for enduring connections. When our words and actions are in harmony, others recognize us as trustworthy individuals. They perceive us as dependable, consistent, and honorable. These traits, grounded in love and truth, forge deep and significant bonds with those around us. People feel secure in the presence of those who embody integrity, knowing there are no hidden agendas or manipulations—just authentic care and respect. This sense of security fosters deeper connections, allowing relationships to thrive in an environment of mutual trust and understanding.

By choosing to live with integrity, we align ourselves with God's divine love and become conduits of its transformative power in the world. Just as a tree bears good fruit by absorbing nutrients from good soil, living with integrity invites us to reflect God's divine love through our actions, uniting us in purpose and purifying our hearts. It signifies a commitment to embody love, patience, kindness, and truth in every aspect of our lives. When we uphold integrity, we transform into vessels of God's love, becoming trustworthy individuals on whom others can rely for guidance and support.

The Ripple Effect of Integrity

A tree does not only benefit itself; it provides shade, fruit, and stability to its surroundings. Likewise, integrity impacts more than just the individual—it influences families, churches, and communities. People trust those who walk in integrity because they know their words and actions align. A life of integrity inspires others to pursue truth and righteousness, creating a ripple effect that transforms relationships and society.

Integrity in leadership fosters trust. Integrity in relationships builds deep, meaningful connections. Integrity in business creates credibility. Every choice to walk in integrity strengthens not only our own lives but also the lives of those around us.

Integrity as a Reflection of God's Character

Integrity is not just a human virtue—it is a reflection of God Himself. Numbers 23:19 declares, "God is not a man, that He should lie." His faithfulness and truthfulness are unchanging. As His children, we are called to mirror His character by being people of integrity in every aspect of our lives. Walking in integrity means that we honor God not only with our words but with our entire being.

Cultivating Integrity in Daily Life

Just as a tree requires nourishment to grow, integrity must be cultivated through intentional daily choices. This includes:

1. **Commitment to truth** – Speaking and living honestly, even when it is difficult.
2. **Accountability** – Surrounding ourselves with people who encourage us to stay on the right path.
3. **Consistency** – Ensuring our actions align with our beliefs, whether in public or private.
4. **Faithfulness in small things** – Integrity is built through small, daily decisions to do what is right.

Love, Integrity, and a Life that Never Fails

At its core, integrity is a reflection of God's unchanging love. Love "always protects, always trusts, always hopes, always perseveres." A person of integrity does the same—they protect truth, inspire trust, hold onto hope, and endure with unwavering faith. A life rooted in love and integrity never fails because it is built on the eternal foundation of God's truth.

Conclusion: Embracing Integrity in a Divided World

Integrity is a bold and countercultural decision. Living with integrity demands bravery. Yet, when we are rooted and grounded in love, integrity flourishes, producing a life that is steadfast, fruitful, and honoring to God. When we absorb integrity into our hearts from the rich soil of God's love and align our vision, purpose, and passion with our core values, we experience a sense of inner peace and clarity. This allows us to navigate the complexities of life with confidence and grace. We transform into individuals who are complete, united, and resolute in our dedication to what is good, true, and beautiful. In doing so, we become beacons of hope in a fragmented world, demonstrating that it is possible to live authentically and purposefully.

May we each strive to be people of integrity, unwavering in our purpose and passion, reflecting the love of Christ in all we do. For in the end, when we are firmly planted in the rich soil of God's love, we will stand strong, unwavering, and fruitful, to the glory of God.

Author
Kecia Reed

Dr. Kecia J. Reed is an empowering leader, Apostle, life counselor, soul therapist, and serial entrepreneur. As the founder and pastor of God's House of Refuge in Suffolk, Virginia, she combines academic excellence with spiritual insight to guide others on their healing and transformational journeys. With a Doctorate of Divinity and a Bachelor's in Pastoral Counseling, Dr. Reed is deeply committed to helping individuals navigate life's complexities through compassionate guidance and holistic healing.

As CEO of Sistas Can We Talk and Reed Solutions, Dr. Reed is a passionate advocate for personal empowerment and spiritual awakening. Known as "Coach Key," she specializes in trauma recovery, emotional healing, and aligning beliefs with divine purpose. Through one-on-one counseling, workshops, and community outreach, she creates safe spaces for clients to uncover their true potential and embrace their authentic selves.

Dr. Reed is also a published author and a dedicated wife, mother, grandmother, and community leader. She believes in the transformative power of faith, self-awareness, and resilience, and is committed to guiding others toward spiritual growth, joy, and peace. Empowered to empower, Dr. Reed is making a lasting impact on the lives of those she serves.

Chapter 7
THE NUTRIENT OF RESILIENCE

"Love endures all things."
(1 Corinthians 13:7)

"Hello from the other side...," Adele's expressive melody resonated within my soul. My mother's diagnosis of dementia shattered my world and plunged me into a darkness I never knew existed. My mom's battle with dementia has been a journey through grief, a slow, agonizing goodbye while she remained physically present.

This vibrant, intelligent, loving, and nurturing woman, who had shaped my life and knew my heart better than anyone, was literally fading before me. Now, she looks at me with eyes that flicker with recognition of me as her daughter, only to quickly be replaced by confusion.

How was I supposed to feel? Not knowing or understanding the implications of this deadly disease. Surely my hero would overcome this as she had with cancer. The diagnosis, the symptoms, and now the manifested fruit of its progression- the confusion, the bursts of aggression, the fear, the loss of cognitive function, the loss of memory and memories. Oh God, hear my heart's cry from the other side. The tears stem from the pain of not knowing, but also of feeling hopeless. As her daughter and her friend, I feel completely dejected. Where do I go for help, and whom do I run to?

In the stillness of time, a small voice whispered, "Be still and know I am God" (Psalm 46:10a). Oh, what comfort and love I found in God's word! Being still had now become my new normalcy with every visit. It was the assurance of words that my husband Stan spoke to my heart in a moment of frustration: "Dear, she may not know you by name, but somewhere in her heart she holds you close. " So, know this: she may never call you by name because she doesn't remember you anymore, but you will always remember hers. " The floodgates of sobering tears conceded with a big sigh of "you're so right."

If you have ever watched a loved one succumb to dementia, you understand the unique grief it brings. It's not just the loss of the present, but the slow erasure of the past, the shared stories, the inside jokes, the memories of how we were, and, most importantly, the very essence of who they are- all locked away and inaccessible to those they loved.

For me, the hardest part was reconciling my faith with my reality. Surely, I believed in the power of prayer. James 5:17 states, *"The effectual fervent prayers of a righteous man availeth much."* I have prayed for many, for what I know to have been more serious conditions, and God sustained them; surely, God would answer my cry concerning my mom. As I prayed fervently, believing in the power of healing, my mother's condition continued to deteriorate. It seemed that the more I prayed, the more complex this disease became. I wrestled with doubt, questioning why some prayers were answered while others seemed to fall on deaf ears. The very essence of fear began to grip my heart regarding what the days ahead would hold for my family.

Fear, while very real, felt like it had me trapped in a wave of anxiety forecasted by depression. Hello God, are you listening to my cries? This was the cry of my heart. In those moments, I realized that although my heart was aching and it seemed that nothing was changing, only growing worse for my mom, I found myself searching for reassurance in God's word. I started having those come-to-Jesus meetings with myself, laughing a little, and I began telling myself, "Self, " and my other self responded, "Huh, you must maintain your faith in God's love." No matter what, don't let anything separate you from the love of God. This is what I kept rehearsing over and over again.

Romans 8:35, "who shall separate me from the love of God? Shall tribulation, or disease, or persecution, or famine, or nakedness, or peril or sword? Nothing, not even Dementia. So where was God in all of this? Where was the light in this overwhelming darkness?

The truth is that the light wasn't some distant, unattainable thing; it was there all along, flickering within me, waiting to be rekindled. It resided in those quiet moments of connection with my mom, even when she didn't recognize me. It was in the gentle touch of her hands, the flicker of recognition in her eyes, and her smile that illuminated every room.

Rooted in Love, Growing in Resilience

Ephesians 3:17-19 speaks of being *"rooted and grounded in love."* It's a powerful imagery, a tree standing firm against the fiercest storms because its roots run deep. That's what God's love is, a deep, unshakeable foundation that can withstand any challenge.

I discovered that resilience isn't about avoiding pain but finding strength in it, Selah. It's about choosing to grow, to learn, and to find meaning even amid suffering. It's about allowing God's love to nourish our souls, giving us the strength to endure and navigate the worst of the worst. My heart welcomes the development of resilience rooted and grounded in God's unwavering love.

The Word of God reminds me daily that He is close to the brokenhearted (Psalm 34:18). In moments of despair, when I fight not to scream, "God, you chose the wrong person," I feel God's presence—a quiet comfort that transcends my understanding. Being rooted in God's love doesn't mean the pain will disappear; rather, it becomes my anchor in the storm. Glory to God! It gives me the strength to be present and to cherish every moment of clarity during our time together, affording me the opportunity to offer her love and compassion as the daughter she raised me to be, even when she couldn't remember who I was.

The Birthing Room of Resilience

Resilience is *"the ability to adapt and overcome challenges, or to bounce back from difficult experiences."* In the eyes of many, resilience is often portrayed as external toughness. My son asked, "Mom, are you hurt or injured?" What was he really asking me? As I postured myself in the Birthing Room of Resilience, I had to discover that my mom's struggle with dementia was my injury; it was the very soil that God was using to display my resilience. I realized my pain and hurt caused me to cry out to God, like no other injury in my life: "Lord, I cannot do this on my own, " only for Him to respond, "Do you trust Me?" Yes, Lord, I do. My injury was stirring what was rooted deep inside me. God's love is unfailing and has been proven time and again, and this injury would be no different.

Resilience is unpacked in our life experiences; it appears in opportunities where giving up seems like the best option, avoidance becomes your scapegoat, and running away from it all feels right in the moment. The love of God serves as resilience's trench coat. It's weatherproofed and designed to be worn in all types of storms, hiding your vulnerabilities, wounds, pain, and injuries so that those around you, who need to be impacted by your resilience, will only see God's Love. They are drawn to your strength and stamina and witness your steadfastness and ability to endure your storms (Glory). Resilience keeps you showing up, bandaged up and all. It tends to appear in the birthing room of our situations to remind us that we're stronger than our dilemmas and that God's love for us runs deep. I Peter 5:7 says, "Casting all your cares upon Him; for He careth for you." God beckoned me to give Him all my worries and concerns. It's the breath of God that becomes the wind beneath our wings when we grow faint.

Unshakeable

The dreaded words of Alzheimer's, coupled with hospice, were being discussed among us, and it began to feel as if someone was beating me in the stomach; I had no strength to fight back. Did this terrible disease take a turn for the worse? Surely this can't be happening, Lord! Many people live with this disease, but why did this sound like a death sentence for my mom? After uncontrollable crying spells, I managed to regain my composure and cry out to God. Resilience was becoming increasingly visible to those around me. They watched me, calculating my moves in anticipation of my breaking under pressure. But the resilience of God was on display. I was trusting and leaning on God's strength to get me through one of the worst phases of my life.

Resilience is a nutrient born in the soil of God's love, cultivated through pain, injury, isolation, adversity, confusion, despair, and even death. Ephesians 3:18 speaks to the breadth, length, height, and depth that surpass knowledge. As we navigate life's lessons, it's God's love that runs deep, developing resilience within us. Resilience is not just about enduring; it's about thriving despite our adversities. It's the roots running deep within us that allow you and me to stand strong.

So, when life starts lifting and the shadows of despair seem to loom larger than the light, remember it's your faith that becomes a guiding star. Prayer has always been intrinsically woven into my life, fueling my resilience. It was my prayers that kept me humbly returning to the Father for strength and comfort. In those dark moments of uncertainty, it was in prayer that I felt God's presence constantly reminding me that I was not alone during this difficult journey. Indeed, we all experience moments of despair and may feel as though we could falter, but when we take time to recognize that God has been there all along, it should rekindle our love for the Father. It compels us to say, "If it had not been for the Lord on our side, where would we be?" because our strength is not solely our own; it's rooted in our resilience.

As you face your own challenges, remember that resilience is not the absence of struggle, but the ability to rise again, fueled with love and faith. Hold fast to the belief that, no matter how dark the path may seem, the light of God's love will guide you through.

Hello, from the other side of my life! I miss my mom dearly, and I reminisce often, not just as a survivor but as a testament to the power of resilience. Every passing day, I am in awe of how resilience, as one of God's nutrients, has brought the best out of me. I am taking a stand in faith, knowing that the love of God runs so deep that giving up is no longer an option.

Which side are you standing on today? Maybe you are emotionally, financially, or spiritually in a hard place, feeling as if life has left you holding the short end of the stick. Take heart that God's love will get you to the other side. One of the first things you must do is validate your stand to receive God's love. Yes, you may be hurting and even confused, but He uses those moments to refine and define us because of who we serve and who you are in Him.

In the soil of God's love, we get a chance to recalibrate our lives in a new light. I would have never thought I would be here today in my right mind after losing my mom, but this loss has strengthened my posture in God.

If you are walking a similar path, know that you are not alone. God's love is constant and an anchor in the storm. Root yourself in that love, and you will find the resilience you need to face whatever challenges come your way. The journey may be difficult, but it doesn't define you. You can and will find light in the darkness, hope amid despair, and resilience rooted and grounded in God's love.

Cultivating Resilience

This journey with my mom has taught me the importance of nurturing my spiritual resilience. Learning to surrender my expectations and accept the reality of my mom's illness has been crucial. I haven't given up hope; rather, it has been about releasing control and trusting God's plan.

Gratitude became a key part of cultivating my resilience. I learned to focus on what I'm grateful for instead of dwelling on things I cannot control.

Daily prayer and meditation are not optional but essential for developing resilience. Pray without ceasing and pray in faith, absorb God's nutrient of resilience as you plant your heart in the rich soil of His love.

Authors

Reginal & Shawn Moss

Apostle Dr. R. D. Moss and Lady Shawn Moss are a dynamic ministry duo dedicated to serving the Kingdom of God through their leadership at Point Of Grace Church International of Metro Atlanta. With a foundation of love, integrity, and faith, they have built a transformative ministry that impacts lives both locally and globally.

Point Of Grace Church, known as The City of Grace, is blessed to have Apostle Dr. R. D. Moss as its Founder and Overseer. Apostle Moss is leading this growing movement with unwavering dedication. A true spiritual planter, Apostle Moss is committed to teaching and preaching God's Word with power and practical wisdom, equipping believers to apply Scripture to their daily lives while nurturing future leaders.

Lady Shawn Moss, Executive Pastor and Administrative Operating Officer at Point of Grace, is an anointed preacher, worship leader, author, entrepreneur, and recording artist. She also is founder of LSM Global, a ministry serving Kingdom advancement. Passionate about empowering others, she especially inspires women to embrace their God-given purpose.

Married for 29 years, they are proud parents of six amazing children and remain devoted to fostering a loving, faith-filled community, offering guidance, hope, and spiritual growth to their church family and beyond.

Chapter 8
THE NUTRIENT OF VICTORY

"Love never fails."
(1 Corinthians 13:8a)

There is perhaps no more powerful testament to the strength of divine love than this simple, yet profound declaration: love never fails. In these three words, we find the nutrient of victory—an essential element in the rich soil of God's love that enables believers to stand firm amid life's storms and challenges, bearing fruit that brings glory to the Lord.

The Ultimate Victory of Love

To understand the victory of love, we must first consider what it means for something to never fail. In a world where failure is commonplace—where relationships dissolve, institutions crumble, and even our best human efforts often fall short—the concept of something that never fails seems almost incomprehensible. Yet, this is precisely what Scripture declares about love—not human love in its imperfect form, but divine love (agape) in its purest essence.

According to the Oxford Dictionary, victory signifies the act of defeating an enemy or opponent in a battle, game, or other competition. In the spiritual realm, the battle between love and hate is vividly depicted through the eyes of Apostle Paul in 1 Corinthians 13:1-13. Paul outlines the characteristics and strategies of love, emphasizing that even the most impressive spiritual gifts amount to nothing without love. This charity—this agape love—is the key to victory. It is the power of God's love working in our lives continuously, transforming us from the inside out.

The victory of love is not like worldly victories, which are often temporary and incomplete. Love's victory is comprehensive and eternal. When Paul writes that love never fails, he uses the Greek word "ekpipto," which implies that love never falls away, becomes ineffective, or loses its power. Unlike prophecies that will cease, tongues that will be stilled, and knowledge that will pass away, love remains. It is the one constant in an ever-changing universe, the bedrock upon which all else stands.

Faith, Grace, and Victory

One of the greatest storylines about victory centers on faith and grace. Grace is crucial because it shows us what victory looks like. It not only reveals the appearance of victory but also demonstrates how victory acts, walks, and celebrates. Grace illustrates the power and finality of victory, providing us with extreme clarity about what it means to overcome.

The relationship between grace and victory is inseparable. Victory cannot exist without the overshadowing of grace. Grace has given victory sustainability and power. Just as a mighty oak tree cannot survive without the nutrients in the soil, victory cannot stand without the foundation of grace. Grace appears in the abundance of love and support, showing up and declaring that we have victory in the name of Jesus.

This victory sustains us through the darkest nights and the most challenging circumstances. It stands firm regardless of how things look or feel. When the storms of life rage around us, threatening to uproot us, the nutrient of victory flowing from God's love keeps us grounded. We become like the tree described in Psalm 1:3, "planted by streams of water, which yields its fruit in season and whose leaf does not wither—whatever they do prospers."

Victory in the Valley

It is important to note that victory is not needed where there is no trouble, no valley, no problem. The first face of victory you will see is through the eyes of faith when you are in your valley, storm, or trouble. During these moments, you witness victory, and it shows you complete faith—the assurance that all is well even when circumstances suggest otherwise.

Consider the Shunammite woman in 2 Kings 4. When her son fell ill and died, she responded to inquiries about his condition with a resolute declaration: "It is well." In this story, we witness her speaking victory even though the problem existed. She spoke victory when she should have been planning a funeral, writing a eulogy, or talking to the undertaker. Instead of succumbing to the situation, she declared, "It is well," demonstrating the power of faith-filled words aligned with the never-failing nature of God's love.

The first face of victory will always appear during your greatest troubles, trials, and tribulations. You can see victory if you have faith, and it starts with the fruit of your lips. You must learn to speak it, declare it, and believe it. Your mouth should confirm what your heart believes, performing the necessary actions by saying the words that need to be spoken. There is no greater completed word than the Word of God, and when we cite and speak it, we align ourselves with the victory that is already ours in Christ.

Love: The Vehicle of Victory

Love is the vehicle of victory. Like a mighty chariot, love travels through time and humanity, through men and women from all walks of life. Love is strong, powerful, and unique, expanding itself in everyone's heart and life. Unlike many other virtues and qualities, love can stand alone. It has brought victory to humanity, to every person, through Jesus Christ.

Love is so powerful that it showed up inside of faith, helped us through the spirit of hope, and even remained steadfast at the foot of the cross. Love is what hung Christ on the cross. He would not have died for us if it had not been for love. As Jesus Himself declared, "Greater love has no one than this: to lay down one's life for one's friends" (John 15:13). This supreme act of love secured the ultimate victory over sin and death.

Love gives us the victory we have in our lives. It shows us that despite calamities, trials, and tribulations, love is unique. It brings victory without cost, price, or money to us—though the cost to God was immeasurable. Love is the vehicle for victory. Victory always rides in the spirit of love. Wherever you find love, you will always find the vehicle of victory.

The Road to Victory

The vehicle of victory is driven on the road to victory. Life lived in the fullness of God's love is a victorious driven life. This is not simply a statement but a reality. A life rooted and grounded in love embraces the totality of God's attributes, character, holiness, perfection, and love. This embrace frees you to a life where victory prevails over defeat.

Although life's complexities arise, it is the nutrients of love that fuel your greatest victories. Imagine yourself at the finish line of a race, holding your hands up high, bursting with joyous laughter because you won. You persevered, didn't give up midway, and pushed through obstacles to claim victory. Now take the same perspective and apply it to the spiritual. There is a spiritual fuel called love that latches on to the core of our being, actively pushing us to victory. This is Love's Victory, the wind beneath your wings pushing you forward.

This wind is sometimes like a whisper telling you not to give up or give in because you will win. One thing the enemy wants you to believe is that you can't succeed or that the outcome is defeat. Remember, this is a deceptive trick of the enemy, the great deceiver, trying to convince you that things won't work out for your good.

But Scripture reminds us, "Thanks be to God, who gives us the victory through our Lord Jesus Christ" (1 Corinthians 15:57). The victory is already ours through Christ. Love never fails because Christ's victory never fails. His triumph over sin and death was complete and eternal, securing for us an inheritance that can never perish, spoil, or fade (1 Peter 1:4).

Facing Life's Complexities with Love's Victory

Do not allow the complexity of a situation to convince you that you must just accept defeat. What you see is not what you have to settle for, especially when it does not match up with God's promises for your life. Pause a moment and speak this truth into your atmosphere: "NO! I am not defeated but the enemy is defeated. YES! I am a victorious winner because of the finished victory of Jesus Christ."

Jesus' finished victory is a win that love fought for. Jesus endured pain, shame, and suffering all the way to the Cross. It wasn't for Himself; it was for the world—for you and me. Jesus, crucified on the cross, hung there because of love. He was placed in the grave of a tomb because love placed Him there. Finally, love's victory revealed His glorious resurrection. Jesus rose with all power, demonstrating that love indeed never fails.

Isaiah prophesied, "But he was wounded for our transgressions, he was bruised for our iniquities: the chastisement of our peace was upon him; and with his stripes we are healed" (Isaiah 53:5). This is the power of love's victory—that through Christ's suffering, we find healing, peace, and redemption.

Personal Victories Through Love

Have you ever known someone in a situation they thought was too difficult to endure, too deep, too complicated, or too far gone to end well? Perhaps you've experienced that place yourself. Whatever your position may be, this is your reminder to trust God. Trusting is believing that love's victory will push you across the finish line. Love's victory in Jesus Christ crossed it first, creating open access to Victory after Victory. The wins are limitless; just begin to see it before you physically see it.

Many believers have personally experienced love's victory throughout their lives. There were times they pushed past failure, pain, disappointment, hurt, insecurities, struggles, sickness, and probably so much more. The reality is that some challenges may have been easier than others, but the truly difficult experiences are the ones that struck like a piercing wound. Yet, they made it through—and so can you.

It is prayer, trust, and faith in God that brings us through. It is not easy, but as you continue through life, you understand that these trials are necessary. It is through those times that we truly learn of love's victory and understand the fight to win. Victory, a nutrient of love, sustains the fight to win. And through it all, Love Wins.

The Elixir of Love's Nutrients

There are pure nutrients in 1 Corinthians 13 that act as an elixir to refresh and replenish life even in hard, broken, and sometimes almost dead places. They open your heart to embrace the truth that love truly wins. Love wins because love transforms what seems to be a dead-end situation into a situation with endless possibilities.

Love wins over emptiness and fills every void. It wins over brokenness by making you whole. It puts hope in the face of despair. What seems impossible turns into miraculous victories through the power of love. It may look like a dead end, but open your eyes to see that the place you are in is a place of purpose, a place of destiny. You may not have reached the final point of this place just yet, but as with any race, you must keep going. You won't know where God is taking you unless you continue to run toward His expected end.

The Two Faces of Love on the Road to Victory

There are two sides of love that are faced on the road to victory: the expression of love and the perseverance of love.

The outpouring of love's expression is seen in those joyous moments that fill our hearts with warmth. It is the side that is perceived as blissful and wonderful. It satisfies the taste of love's emotions, felt from heart to heart. The expression of love gives us reassurance and comfort.

There is also the persevering side of love. Perseverance is the side that fights to hold on. It fights to hold on through trials, fights to stay steady, and endures to the end. Perseverance does not give up to challenges nor the people challenged. It is the perseverance of love that makes you try and then try harder, especially when you are working through tough situations. It endures to make it across the winning line.

This path is complicated by a roller coaster of emotions: pain, tears, heartache, sleepless nights, brokenness. The list could go on and on. But on this side of the victory line, love is what love does. As Paul writes, love *"beareth all things, believeth all things, hopeth all things, endureth all things"* (1 Corinthians 13:7). This persevering love never fails—it remains steadfast through every trial and challenge.

Running the Race of Love

In life's race, the conditions are not always optimal. There may be turns, hills, broken roads, ditches, cracks, potholes, rain, and then sunshine every now and then. Nevertheless, it is important to stay in the race and follow the course mapped out from the beginning of your life. You may be tempted to detour down a path that seems easier or even a little smoother, but dismiss that thought and forge forward in the way that God has mapped out.

If you've already detoured, take heart—it's not too late to get back on the right path. Sometimes it may not be an immediate win, but it's worth the wait. Walking in love is a walk in victory. It is a journey that often requires sacrifice, but the triumph of victory is right in front of you.

As you continue your pursuit of victory, embrace the things you need to hold tight and release the things you need to let go. Then make a decision to embrace joy as you cross the finish line to love's victory! Remember the promise in Psalm 30:5, *"Weeping may endure for a night, but joy comes in the morning."*

Love's Victory: Transforming Lives

When we are truly rooted and grounded in love, the nutrient of victory transforms every aspect of our lives. We become like those mighty trees described in Isaiah 61:3, "oaks of righteousness, a planting of the LORD for the display of his splendor." These are not weak, spindly saplings that bend with every wind of adversity, but strong, resilient trees that stand firm through the fiercest storms.

The nutrient of victory manifests in our lives in numerous ways:

1. **Overcoming Fear**: *"There is no fear in love. But perfect love drives out fear"* (1 John 4:18). When love's victory takes root in our hearts, fear loses its grip on our lives.

2. **Conquering Bitterness**: Love's victory enables us to forgive those who have wronged us, releasing us from the prison of bitterness and resentment.

3. **Defeating Pride**: The victory of love humbles us, reminding us that our success is not due to our own strength but to God's grace working through us.

4. **Vanquishing Selfishness**: Love's victory shifts our focus from self-centered concerns to the needs of others, enabling us to serve with joy and generosity.

5. **Overcoming Despair**: Even in our darkest moments, love's victory gives us hope. As Paul declared, *"We are hard pressed on every side, but not crushed; perplexed, but not in despair; persecuted, but not abandoned; struck down, but not destroyed"* (2 Corinthians 4:8-9).

The Never-Failing Victory

As we conclude our exploration of the nutrient of victory, let us remember that love never fails because God never fails. His love is the foundation of our victory, the soil in which we are rooted and grounded. When we abide in His love, drawing daily nourishment from its rich nutrients, we become those trees of righteousness that bear fruit in every season.

The victory of love is not a one-time event but an ongoing reality in the life of every believer. It is a victory that sustains us through trials, empowers us for service, and ultimately brings glory to God. As we continue to grow in love, let us hold fast to the promise that love never fails. In a world of uncertainty and change, this is our anchor, our hope, and our victory.

Let us go forth as bearers of love's victory, demonstrating to a broken world that there is a love that never fails, a victory that cannot be defeated, and a God who remains faithful through every circumstance. For when we are rooted and grounded in love, we become living testimonies to the transformative power of the greatest nutrient of all—the never-failing victory of divine love.

"But thanks be to God! He gives us the victory
through our Lord Jesus Christ."
— 1 Corinthians 15:57

CONCLUSION
ROOTED AND GROUNDED IN LOVE

As we come to the end of our journey through the first eight nutrients found in the rich soil of God's love, we stand in awe of the transformation that takes place when we allow ourselves to be truly rooted and grounded in His perfect love. The apostle Paul's prayer in Ephesians 3:17 reveals a profound truth: our spiritual growth depends entirely on how deeply our roots extend into the nourishing love of Christ.

Throughout these pages, we have explored how love's patience teaches us to endure with grace, mirroring God's longsuffering toward us. We've seen how kindness flows naturally from hearts connected to the Source of all compassion. We've discovered that true generosity emerges when we, like our Savior, seek not our own but the welfare of others.

The peace that comes from love—a peace that is not easily provoked—has shown us the power of remaining steadfast amid life's storms. Forgiveness has revealed itself as the choice to think no evil, to release others from the debt of their offenses just as Christ has released us. We've witnessed how integrity rejoices in truth, standing firm on God's Word even when the world embraces deception.

The resilience of love—enduring all things—has demonstrated how deeply rooted trees withstand the fiercest winds of adversity. And finally, we've celebrated the ultimate victory of love that never fails, even when all else fades away.

These eight nutrients, when absorbed into our spiritual DNA, transform us from saplings vulnerable to every gust of worldly influence into mighty oaks of righteousness, planted by the Lord for His glory (Isaiah 61:3). But the transformation is not instantaneous. Just as a tree grows slowly, often imperceptibly, so too does our character develop through seasons of sunshine and rain, through gentle breezes and howling winds.

The beauty of being rooted and grounded in love is that our growth is not dependent on our own strength or willpower. Rather, it relies on our willingness to remain connected to the Source. Jesus reminded us in John 15:5, *"I am the vine; you are the branches. If you remain in me and I in you, you will bear much fruit; apart from me you can do nothing."* Our fruitfulness—our ability to manifest patience, kindness, generosity, peace, forgiveness, integrity, resilience, and victory—flows directly from our connection to Him.

As we prepare to explore the remaining eight nutrients in the next volume, let us pause to assess the depth of our roots. Are we merely skimming the surface of God's love, or have we allowed our roots to penetrate deeply into His unfathomable grace? Are we drawing daily nourishment from His Word and presence, or are we attempting to sustain ourselves on the insufficient resources of our own making?

The invitation stands before us each day: to sink our roots ever deeper into the soil of divine love. This is not a passive process but an intentional one. Just as trees extend their roots in search of water, we must actively seek God's presence, creating space in our busy lives for communion with Him. As we do, we find ourselves becoming more like Him—more patient, more kind, more generous, more peaceful, more forgiving, more truthful, more resilient, and more victorious.

Remember that the ultimate purpose of our growth is not self-improvement or personal happiness, though these may be byproducts. Rather, it is to bring glory to the Lord by bearing fruit that reflects His character to a world desperately in need of genuine love. As Jesus told His disciples, *"This is to my Father's glory, that you bear much fruit, showing yourselves to be my disciples"* (John 15:8).

As we close this first volume, may Paul's prayer become our own daily aspiration: that Christ would dwell in our hearts through faith, and that we, *"being rooted and grounded in love, may be able to comprehend with all the saints what is the width and length and depth and height—to know the love of Christ which passes knowledge; that you may be filled with all the fullness of God"* (Ephesians 3:17-19).

The journey continues, beloved. May your roots grow ever deeper into the boundless love of Christ, and may your branches reach heavenward in worship to the One who first loved us.

NOTES
The Nutrient of Patience

NOTES
The Nutrient of Kindness

_____

_____

_____

_____

_____

_____

_____

_____

_____

_____

_____

_____

_____

_____

_____

_____

_____

_____

_____

NOTES
The Nutrient of Generosity

_____

_____

_____

_____

_____

_____

_____

_____

_____

_____

_____

_____

_____

_____

_____

_____

_____

_____

_____

_____

NOTES
The Nutrient of Peace

_____

_____

_____

_____

_____

_____

_____

_____

_____

_____

_____

_____

_____

_____

_____

_____

_____

NOTES
The Nutrient of Forgiveness

NOTES
The Nutrient of Integrity

_____

_____

_____

_____

_____

_____

_____

_____

_____

_____

_____

_____

_____

_____

_____

_____

_____

_____

_____

NOTES
The Nutrient of Resilience

_____

_____

_____

_____

_____

_____

_____

_____

_____

_____

_____

_____

_____

_____

_____

_____

_____

_____

_____

_____

_____

NOTES
The Nutrient of Victory

www.ingramcontent.com/pod-product-compliance
Lightning Source LLC
Chambersburg PA
CBHW051228120626
46547CB00013B/1556